CHURCH UNION

A Layman's Guide

by
ROBERT P. LIGHTNER, TH.D.

Assistant Professor of Systematic Theology
Dallas Theological Seminary
Dallas, Texas

REGULAR BAPTIST PRESS
1800 Oakton Boulevard
Des Plaines, Illinois 60018

Library of Congress Catalog Card Number: 72-176318

Printed in the United States of America

To the memory of
Dr. Paul R. Jackson
whose dedicated Christian life
and personal counsel
have been of inestimable value
to me in things spiritual.

CONTENTS

FOREWORD

The most dangerous and complicated situation which faces the true church of Jesus Christ today is to be found in the National and the World Councils of Churches. The danger and complication resident in these two Councils is intensified by the friendly and compromising attitude of the New Evangelical group, which advocates cooperation with much of the program of these Councils.

The laymen and laywomen in our churches need to know about this church union toward which these Councils are rapidly moving. Pastors are familiar with these dangers because their mails are flooded with propaganda literature. The laity, however, does not receive most of this literature and is, therefore, unaware of the specific evil which it faces.

The idea of a "One World Church" looks good, but it is wholly evil when it is accomplished. Dr. Lightner goes at once to the heart of the matter. He does so in plain and simple language which the layman can understand. The opening chapter of his book presents a clear and understandable picture of this apostate juggernaut as it moves relentlessly to crush every fundamental and truly Biblical work which stands in the way of its ultimate accomplishment.

The third chapter describes clearly the historic development of these anti-Christian Councils. The entire book is an exceptional presentation of the whole destructive program of these Councils. It should be read by every layman who loves his Lord and his church.

Let us face the facts. Is Jesus Christ the virgin-born Son of God? Is the Bible the inerrant and holy Word of God? If so, then everything has an answer and is settled! If not, then nothing is answered and nothing is settled.

Neither the National nor World Councils of Churches believes that Christ is the virgin-born Son of God. Neither do they believe that the Bible is the inerrant and inspired Word of God. Therefore, their programs and objectives leave nothing answered and nothing settled so far as man's relation to a holy God is concerned.

Dr. Lightner shows with unerring accuracy just how true and awful this situation is. Every true Christian owes it to himself to be informed as to the facts, lest he be caught up in the judgments of God when, some day, He will call this apostate church to answer for its blasphemy concerning the Son of God and the Word of God.

A copy of this book should be in every Christian home. These are days of confusion in matters pertaining to the church and its ministry. This book clearly presents the whole perplexing picture in understandable language. It throws the light of infallible Scripture upon the ecumenical maze and offers the only remedy by which an individual born-again Christian can find his way out of it.

Robert T. Ketcham, D.D., LL.D.
Former National Representative and
National Consultant of the General
Association of Regular Baptist Churches

ACKNOWLEDGMENTS

Much of what appears in these pages was presented originally to the students of the San Francisco Baptist Theological Seminary, San Francisco, California. Selected portions of the work also appeared earlier in the following periodicals: *The Discerner, Christian News,* and *Voice* (official organ of the Independent Fundamental Churches of America).

The author wishes to express appreciation to many who made valuable contributions to this work by supplying needed information. A special word of thanks belongs to my wife, Pearl, for typing the manuscript and offering helpful suggestions and to Mr. James Scott, Assistant Librarian, Dallas Theological Seminary, Dallas, Texas, for preparing the indices.

I

SURVEYING THE SCENE

Whether one is for it or against it, the modern attempt toward church union is a reality. In recent years and even months and days the movement has grown tremendously. At a phenomenal pace the ecumenical idea is spreading and engulfing more and more denominations and groups. The drive for church union, for a worldwide church, has become the burning passion of the majority of church leaders today. Efforts of the ecumenical leaders and church councils cannot be ignored by the layman. After all, it is his church which is the target of the ecumenists and which is being destroyed. What kind of a church will remain in which he can rear his family? Will the church of the future be worthy of the name? Will his children be taught in the historic orthodox Christian faith, the faith of our fathers, the faith once delivered to the saints? Matters such as these ought to concern the layman. They should be uppermost in his thinking. He ought to know that the ecumenical enthusiasts are seeking to pull the proverbial wool over his eyes. Through a conditioning process those pressing for church union expect the man in the pew who

is at all concerned with his church and has any evangelical lean-
ings to become insensitive to what is really happening. Then by
the time it happens to his church, and others like his, he is
supposed to think it is all a work of God.

W. A. Visser 't Hooft, who was General Secretary of the
World Council of Churches from 1948 to 1966 and was made
Honorary President in 1968, recently surveyed the ecumenical
developments from their beginning to the present. Speaking of
the periods of development he said: "The first had been the
period of the pioneers. . . . The second period was that of the
architects who sought to give a more clearly defined shape to the
ecumenical movement. . . . The year 1948 marked the beginning
of the third period. A new generation took over. . . . The task
was now to ensure that the ecumenical movement should really
become ecumenical, that it should become the ecumenical movement of the Churches, and that it should develop adequate
structures. . . . The story of the years since 1948 is essentially the
story of the process through which the ecumenical movement
became universalized. It is a story of ecumenical mobilization of
practically all Christian Churches."[1]

Even the average unchurched American is plagued with much
uncertainty concerning the future because of the tremendous
revolutionary changes sweeping our society. Walter Lippman, a
political commentator, stated in *Newsweek* for September 23,
1968, " . . . we are now living in a time when the central institutions of the traditional life of man are increasingly unable to
command his allegiance and his obedience. The family, whatever its future, is profoundly shaken and is no longer able to be
the disciplinary power that it has been in the past. The church
is confused by the cosmic demonstrations made by science and is
in an acute crisis of belief as to how to conduct its teaching
functions." The secular press frequently reports on the doubt
and denial of orthodox doctrine so prevalent today among the
clergy. *Time* magazine, November 11, 1966, reported the doubt
and denial of such basic doctrines as original sin, the virgin birth
of Christ, the Trinity and the resurrection of Christ from the

---

[1] *The Ecumenical Advance — A History of the Ecumenical Movement,
1948-1968*, Volume 2, edited by Harold E. Fey, pp. 3, 4.

grave. The same account listed James Albert Pike, former Episcopal bishop of California and now deceased, as the most visible of the doubters. Church members and the general public are being told that clergymen today have a "new role." A feature article in *U.S. News and World Report* reveals examples of this new clergy role. In Milwaukee a Roman Catholic priest led Negroes in an open-housing drive, and he condoned the violence that resulted. Two Detroit pastors offered their churches as havens for draft-dodgers. In San Francisco ministers walked through hippie colonies praising teen-agers for their use of "pot" which they said was a contemporary version of early Christianity. Harvey Cox of Harvard Divinity School and occasional speaker for the National Council of Churches has given great impetus to this new breed of clergymen in his book, *The Secular City.*

McCall's magazine in February, 1968 reported the widespread confusion and disbelief in the pulpits. The report was the result of a survey of three thousand Protestant clergymen concerning their theological beliefs. The *McCall's* article stated, "A considerable number rejected altogether the idea of a personal God. God, they said, was 'the Ground of Being,' 'the Force of Life,' 'the Principle of Love,' 'Ultimate Reality' and so forth. A majority of the youngest group cannot be said to believe in the Virgin Birth or to regard Jesus as divine in the traditional way in which most Protestants were brought up."

Newspapers, secular magazines, and almost all modern means of news media have been giving considerable coverage to the present-day movement toward church union. From every quarter there is news of the ecumenical movement. If the wise Solomon had lived in the twentieth century the Spirit of God probably would have led him to write, "Of the making of ecumenical books there is no end."

Because of the pressure of church unionists those who embrace the historic orthodox faith and thus oppose the church-union movement have been forced to create their own means for being heard. Major media of communication seem to wish to report only news which emanates from sources approved by councils and groups involved in the church-union movement. They are either altogether closed to the opposing views or are so disinterested in them that they rarely give them more than scant mention. Usually, only the side of the ecumenical liberal establishment is heard. No doubt the Councils of Churches and similar organizations are responsible for this since they claim to speak for Protestantism. Many evangelical churches and groups have thus banded together to produce Bible-centered publications— Christian periodicals, books, Sunday school and church materials. They have also sought to stifle the attempted monopoly which the National Council of Churches desires over radio and television. Some years ago an attempt was made to bind all the major national radio outlets in a contract which would give the Council the control. This attempt failed when the National Religious Broadcasters Incorporated took the matter to the Federal Communications Commission in the name of free speech. Evangelicals have also built independent and privately owned radio stations so that the truth may be heard.

The ecumenists, those who are strongly pushing for the union of all religious groups into one world church, have been producing many volumes promoting the ecumenical movement. Evangelicals who have serious reservations and óbjections to the movement have also produced a few notable critiques. However, very few volumes have been written with the layman in view. The layman deserves to know what is happening to his church. He needs to know what the drive for church union is all about and what the net result will be if and when the ecumenists' goal is reached. The bill of goods which he is being sold needs to be exposed thoroughly in his language so that he can understand it and have a firm basis for an intelligent decision regarding his own relationship to it. This book is̓ designed to help meet this need.

The word *ecumenical,* according to W. A. Visser 't Hooft, past General Secretary of the World Council of Churches, refers to "that quality or attitude which expresses the consciousness of and desire for. Christian unity." The word at one time meant "pertaining to the whole earth." Later it came to mean "pertaining to the whole church." At the present time it is usually used to describe the desire for the union of all religious groups into one church. Thus as the term is used to describe the present movement within professing Christendom it means worldwide cooperation and fellowship among all religious bodies regardless of doctrinal agreement. "Unionism" was the term which was previously used to describe this attempt. The purposes and goals of those seeking church union have not changed; only the language used to describe their efforts has been altered.

The modern movement toward church union is not attacking the evils of the day. Instead it is waging an all-out war against the historic orthodox Christian faith. What is even more alarming is this sad fact: As more and more evangelical individuals and churches become duped by the dishonest double-talk of the leaders of church union (ecumenists), the war against the faith once delivered to the saints is being expanded by the church wolves who appear in sheep's clothing. Sad is the day when the people in the pew must rise up and cry for the proclamation of the truth from the pulpit.

Absolutes and truth are being denied more and more in our modern age. All phases of modern education either soft-pedal or candidly deny the existence of, and therefore the possibility of understanding, absolute truth. We are being told that there is no such thing as truth and error. Things are not either right or wrong, black or white; everything is a muddy gray. The novel and unique feature of this widespread denial is that the clergymen are among the most outspoken and prominent deniers of the Bible as ultimate and absolute truth from God. They engage in undermining the historic Christian faith in most subtle and insidious ways. While they pretend to be defending the faith they are in fact destroying it.

The drive for church union, like most other evils which plague the church, did not begin in the pew. Heresy has never begun on the lay level. It always starts at the top and then filters down. Denominational leaders of the upper echelon are responsible for the movement. In fact, the theological deterioration which accompanies the ecumenical movement began in the educational centers of learning. From there it very naturally entered the pulpits of the churches. And, of course, when the man in the pulpit has been affected it is not very long until the majority of the people in the pew are conditioned slowly, but ever so surely, to accept the ecumenical line.

All the major Protestant denominations were taken over by the liberal establishment in precisely the same way. The theological liberal needs only the proverbial inch and he will soon take the proverbial mile. Many modern pastors, denominational leaders and theologians are directing their zeal and efforts against historic orthodoxy. Instead of fulfilling their divine responsibility of protecting the people who look to them for spiritual guidance from dangerous error, they are busying themselves with trying to bring the church down to the level of the unchurched. The constant cry of the liberal church minister is to make the gospel relevant and to get the church and Christians involved with the social needs of men and with all the other current issues which are clamoring for attention. We are being told that the church must become more worldly, must become more involved in social action. All the while this is being done, the proclamation of the Word of God and the rebuke of individual sin goes by the board. Churchmen are more and more involving their churches in civil affairs. Those enamored with church union are leading the church farther and farther away from the salvation of the individual to the reformation of the individual and of society. An active and distinguished church layman voiced the sentiment of many alert laymen when he said, "I am concerned that many of the church's top leaders today—especially in what are called the 'mainstream' denominations—are sorely failing their members in two ways: (1) by succumbing to a creeping tendency to downgrade the Bible as the infallible Word of God, and 2) by efforts to shift the church's main thrust from the spiritual to the secular. The two, I believe, are related."[2]

Little wonder that a Gallup Poll shows a steady decline in church attendance when simultaneously there is a steady rise in church membership. The "message" delivered on a given Sunday morning from the pulpit of the average American church is often hardly more than a lecture attempting to convince the listener of his own abilities for decision-making and his need to become in-

---

[2]J. Howard Pew, "Should the Church Meddle in Civil Affairs?" *Reader's Digest* (May, 1966).

volved in the world situation. The "Thus saith the Lord" of the Scriptures has been discarded long ago by countless numbers of the contemporary clergy. To fill the vacuum created by the abandonment of an authoritative Word from God there has come the feverish desire to get the church involved in areas beyond its God-ordained jurisdiction. As a result of this shift of emphasis there has come the loss of winning individuals to Christ and in its place an attempt to evangelize the structures of society.

Laymen are justified in becoming indignant when a church or church council pretends and even purports to speak for the entire membership when it addresses the social, economic, and political issues of the day. It is common today to read or hear of clergymen defying police barriers, protesting America's military involvements, condemning prayers in public schools and even sanctioning promiscuity and homosexuality. At no time in history has the professing church been more decadent than it is today. The desperate plight of the professing church did not suddenly develop. Through a long, slow process, little by little, the laymen have been conditioned to accept the liberal line.

No serious-minded Christian would deny the need to apply and relate his Christianity to everyday life and to the needs of society. Likewise there would be little, if any, objection to the right and the responsibility of the preacher to speak out on all matters which involve spiritual and moral issues. But when the church forsakes its role and seeks to pressure its members and the state and federal government into action which is foreign to its God-ordained duties, it has no right to pawn off such action as a part of the responsible worship of God. Even civil authorities and lawmakers are sickened and saddened by the church's involvement in affairs that are not a part of its responsibility.

Why is there such a reckless drive for church union today? What is it that causes the ecumenical leaders to wish to build a world church? What are the motivations of the ecumenists for church union? It is difficult to find specific reasons given by the ecumenists themselves. However, hidden behind a barrage of words several reasons can be uncovered. All of these are related or are the direct result of the rejection of the Bible as the infallible Word of God and of Christ as God. They follow very naturally upon these basic problems.

Though church unionists would not admit it, one gets the impression through their writings and lectures that many of them have a personal passion for power and prestige. There is evident a lust for power. Of course, that sin is not only present among ecumenists. It crops up all too often among evangelicals as well. The language of the church-union leaders is also filled with emphasis upon the divided world in which we live. Ecumenists feel that a united church under one central organization could effect a control and dominate world affairs so that they would be directed toward more worthy ends. Church unionists want the church to exert force and pressure on the government. The net result of such action would, of course, be the breakdown of that Biblical principle of separation of church and state. In such a case the church would virtually control the state. We are being told too that God intends that there be a single united ecclesiastical structure. This is what Christ prayed for in His high-priestly prayer recorded in John 17, say the ecumenists. And this also, they say, is what the Apostle Paul meant when he said, "There is one body. . . " (Eph. 4:4-6). Then those who desire to see a world church often remind us that a divided church will never be able to make an impact upon the heathen world. In fact, they insist that Christianity will never be plausible or attractive to nonchristians in its present divided state. The entire ecumenical movement is based upon the idea that all division and separateness is sin and is therefore contrary to God's will. We shall have more to say about this later.

Now these all sound like worthy and noble reasons until the theology and beliefs of the ecumenists are examined. Since they have rejected the Bible as the infallible Word of God, it follows that the church, the testimony to the heathen, and the unity and the Christ of which they speak have no relationship to the Scriptures. How strange, contradictory, and paradoxical it is that the very ones who have candidly and forthrightly repudiated the final authority of the Bible want to turn to it for support for their anti-biblical views. The deceptive efforts of church unionists must be revealed and exposed. Many laymen who are deceived with the teaching and tactics of the ecumenical leaders are led astray. They trust their church and its leadership and therefore believe what is promoted in the name of Christianity. Honesty must prevail! The liberal ecumenical church-union leaders cannot be trusted. They engage in much double-talk. Talking out of both sides of their mouths, they with one breath discredit the Bible and with the next breath want to find refuge in the Bible for their movement.

Leaders of the National Council and World Council of Churches, which organizations are the chief proponents of church union, cleverly engage in the use of the language of orthodoxy while investing it with new and foreign meanings. This act is known as semantic delusion. They are also wise enough to know that if they are going to win to their side and to the cause of church union those who are evangelical in the faith and those who are on the borderline between historic orthodoxy and modern theology, they must in some way appeal to such. To do this, evangelical speakers are often invited to their platforms. This provides an attitude of broad inclusivism. It appeases the consciences of those in the ecumenical movement who are convicted by their affiliations. The sad and regrettable thing is that when such an invitation is extended to an evangelical spokesman and he accepts, he usually waters down the message, seeks to remove the offense of the Cross and minimizes the glaring differences between his professed beliefs and the well-publicized views of the ecumenists. Even the secular press writers are aware of such attempts. For example, *Time* magazine reported how Billy Graham succeeded in synthesizing his view of evangelism with those of the National Council of Churches when he spoke in Miami at the National Council of Churches conference in December 1966, " . . . where one third of the delegates could not even give unqualified belief in the reality of God, the divinity of Jesus, or life after death."[3] Many evangelicals seriously question the wisdom and the Biblical basis for such a synthesizing of views.

The ideal form of church union would be for all those who reject the absolute authority of the Bible, regardless of their re-

---

[3]See News Report in *Christianity Today*, June 21, 1967.

ligious label, and who therefore repudiate historic orthodox Christianity to accurately label their movement and form one great organization. No Bible-believing Christian could, or at least should, object to that king of "church" union. What is lamentable though and what everyone who loves the Word of God should object to is the inclusion of believers with unbelievers in such an attempt and the dishonest widespread claim of the ecumenical movement to be speaking for and on behalf of all the churches and the Christians in them. Yet, this is precisely what is being done in the drive for church union and it is being done in the name of Christianity.

Perhaps the most deceptive device of the ecumenists is to take proof texts from the Bible, whose authority they reject, to defend their action and goal! Of course the ecumenists are famous for making light of this method when it is used by the evangelicals. This is an extremely subtle move on their part. Many laymen who are not familiar with the doctrinal beliefs and goals of the ecumenists but who do give some allegiance to the Scriptures therefore accept the ecumenical movement as Biblical and as the means for the fulfillment of what the ecumenists say is God's intended purpose for the church. On the surface of things it would appear to those unfamiliar with God's program that the union of all religious bodies into one church would be a means of righting many wrongs and of providing a united effort for the propagation of the gospel. There is a lot of needless competition of churches. Overlapping and duplicating efforts at home and abroad is surely taking place among those who profess to be Christ's followers. In a subsequent chapter we will deal with the matter of whether division is sin. We will observe also whether the church unionists have demonstrated that the measure of union they have thus far achieved has resulted in the multiplication of the spread of the good news and the increase of the church or simply the stifling of it and its outreach.

There are two texts of Scripture which those pushing for church union frequently use to defend their action. Of these John 17:21 is used most often: "That they all may be one; as thou, Father, art in me, and I in thee, that they also may be one in us: that the world may believe that thou hast sent me." Liberal churchmen have ripped this verse completely from its setting and have used it as a slogan to highlight all their efforts and to corral all religious groups under one roof into a united church. They speak much about "the unity we seek" and they claim as a basis for such unity this prayer of Christ. These texts and the claims of the ecumenists will be discussed subsequently.

This book seeks to answer some pertinent questions regarding the current ecumenical movement. The author's firm conviction is that the movement rests on some tremendously erroneous concepts and premises. There is a colossal failure on the part of its proponents to distinguish between the Church and the churches, between the true Body of Christ and professing Christendom. A totally subjective, man-centered theology forms the basis of those crying for church union. A widespread rejection of the infallible authority of the Bible characterizes them. The ecumenical movement assumes and insists that the best possible thing that could happen would be the union of all churches into one religious structure. Those spearheading the movement also insist that church division and denominationalism are scandalous sins. The Protestant Reformation, in their minds, was a stupendous mistake. To them, church union is of the highest priority and to promote it they miserably distort portions of Scripture thus making their error appear to be Biblically based.

This book is intended to be a sincere warning to those involved and engulfed in the ecumenical movement. The author's prayer is that some eyes will be opened to the danger and deception of the ecumenical movement. For those in the valley of decision this volume is also intended. Multitudes make up this company. They do not know what to do. The whole movement does not seem quite right; yet they are confused and uncertain as to what their relationship should be to their own church and its involvements. Finally, it is hoped that that band of believers who have courageously taken their stand against the movement, have severed all relations with the ecumenical drive and have become part of a Bible-believing and preaching testimony will find help and encouragement from these pages.

II

THEOLOGICAL BACKGROUND

How did the modern idea of church union get started? Much can be gained in understanding the current ecumenical movement which is receiving such widespread publicity even in the secular press when its historical and theological background is known. It all started with the rise of theological liberalism which was born in and grew out of the man-centered philosophies of the Renaissance and the periods which followed. There were always threats to Biblical Christianity, but those which began around the fifteenth century and found their origin in humanistic philosophy attacked the historic Christian faith from without.

Faith in man was the cry of the Renaissance (1453-1690). Philosophers of this period had a profound interest in this world. A genuine faith in reason and the capabilities of man in this life crowded out virtually all interest in God and His revelation to man. Without making a concerted and dedicated attempt to overthrow Biblical Christianity the philosophers of the day succeeded in introducing a complete and widespread skepticism of the Bible. God and the Bible were dethroned. Man was elevated and became the standard and norm of truth.

With the passing of time and the introduction of more philosophers, the attacks against Christianity became stronger and stronger. Though most of these men maintained some sort of belief in God, their students and those who were exposed to their philosophies soon realized, as Immanuel Kant did, that the existence of God could not be proven or demonstrated rationally. The natural corollary of this course was the rejection of the miraculous and all the great Biblical doctrines of the faith and then the inspiration and authority of the Bible itself.

These secular philosophers had a direct influence upon the theologians who started theological liberalism. Friedrich Daniel Schleiermacher has rightly been called "the father of liberalism." Born in Germany in 1768 and influenced greatly by the humanistic philosophies, he founded his authority, not in the mind of man as the philosophers had done, but in the soul's experiences. Along with many of his contemporaries, he rejected the Bible as the authoritative revelation of God to man. Schleiermacher introduced a theology of feeling. For him, Christianity was not revealed in a set of propositions recorded in a book called the Bible, but by an inner feeling or experience. Subjective feeling was his source of authority rather than objective fact. This meant that all the Biblical terminology concerning doctrine was invested with new meaning. Soon many others became enamored with the views of Schleiermacher. They saw 'his views as an inviting alternative to the purely rationalistic philosophies before him. In one sense, Schleiermacher and his followers were reacting against the purely rationalistic approach of the day. Yet they were by no means returning to the authority of Holy Writ for their views. With the passing of time scholars began to assimilate and combine elements of rationalism and the theology of feeling of Schleiermacher. They addressed themselves to the Bible. At first the Gospels were attacked as many of the features of historic Christianity and the findings of the philosophers were combined. Very naturally human reason soon became the determining factor in deciding what was and what was not the Word of God. Whereas the Bible once stood over man as Judge, now man was standing over the Bible as its judge. What had been done to the Gospels and the rest of the New Testament was soon done to the Old Testament.

Science added its weight to that of philosophy and theology attempting to make Christianity untenable. The discoveries of science made the earth and man appear as very unimportant. Charles Darwin's book, *The Origin of Species,* in 1859 succeeded in bringing doubt and disrepute upon the Bible, especially the first few chapters of Genesis. Theologians who rejected the authority of Scripture and accepted Darwin's evolutionary hypothesis introduced what has come to be known as higher criticism. This was simply the application of Darwin's theory of evolution and the survival of the fittest to the Bible. Those who applied this method to the Bible sought to discover the origin of ideas set forth in Scripture. They also attempted to determine at what points the Bible was true and at what points it was false. Theologians who accepted the findings of the higher critics and who were sympathetic to them were occupying places of prominence in Europe. Many students from America went abroad for theological education. Naturally as they studied under these men and in this liberal influence they imbibed much of what they were taught. Returning to America these men brought their theological liberalism with them and found the climate in this country quite receptive to them. The "Christianity" which they proclaimed and promoted in their pulpits and positions of Christian leadership was diametrically opposed to the historic Christian faith. The cardinal doctrines of the faith were candidly and forthrightly rejected. For many of them the Bible was composed of nothing but myths and legends. The inspiration of the Bible was boldly rejected and redefined in terms of the human author rather than what was written. Such unbelief was only the natural result of applying the scientific method to the Bible. The liberal theologians tried to put God in a test tube and ruled out as mythological what He had said in His Word. One extreme of unbelief led to another. Even the actual existence of Jesus in space-time history was doubted by many. The early church, it was said, invented the Jesus myth. This kind of rejection represented the liberal theology of the nineteenth century, especially in Europe.

In America the influence of such unbelief was also being

felt. Many were questioning and rejecting the great tenets of the faith. Even the basic fundamentals of the faith stressed by the Reformers were being denied. The sole authority of the Scriptures and salvation by faith alone were being compromised and denied. The Great Awakening, spearheaded by Jonathan Edwards and George Whitefield, was a reaction to the theological liberalism which had crept into the churches. The worth of man was being preached instead of the Biblical doctrine of the exceeding sinfulness of man.

Shortly after the revivals of the Great Awakening the denial of the doctrine of the Trinity, the deity of Christ, and of course the authority of the Bible followed. Even though the revivals did not stop the spread of liberal theology, they did stem its tide temporarily. The word and writings of Horace Bushnell and Walter Rauschenbush with their emphasis upon the "social gospel" soon spread widely and became the liberal rallying point. Through the propagation of the "social gospel" the liberals denied the Biblical doctrine of man's sinfulness and concentrated their efforts upon making the world a better place in which to live. They emphasized the idea of a coming utopia or kingdom brought about through human effort. After the world was cured of all sin the kingdom would be established through man's endeavor. Liberals sincerely believed and preached that the world was becoming better and better. The successful industrialization which was taking place at the time aided the contention of the liberal spokesmen.

Liberal churchmen, who had already denied the major tenets of the faith, endeavored to unite churches into large bodies so their cause could be promoted on a wide scale. The National Federation of Churches and Christian Workers, formed in 1901, was an example of such an effort. Growing out of that organization in 1908 was the Federal Council of Churches which was under liberal leadership and promoted the liberal doctrines and gave particular stress to the "social gospel," the doctrines of the universal fatherhood of God and the brotherhood of man. In 1948 the World Council of Churches was formed giving worldwide impetus to the drive for church union. The Federal Council of Churches became the National Council of Churches in 1950.

More will be said about these organizations later. Reaction to the old liberal theology came from various quarters. Fundamentalists were not the only ones who found fault with liberalism. Even the unchurched humanists reacted. They insisted, and very logically, that if the liberal churchmen were right in their view of God, man, sin, and salvation, there was little or no need for any revelation from God. Carried to their logical conclusion the liberal doctrines ruled out completely any need for the Bible. Man could get along just as well without it. Also, the First World War was a reaction to the liberal belief in a golden age, a utopia, about to be ushered in by human efforts. What more devastating reply to the liberal doctrines of man's goodness and his establishment of a kingdom could there be than the bloody war?

In response to the reactions against the old liberal theology and the destructive effects of both World Wars and their aftermaths, liberal churchmen restructured their system of belief and reworded their rejection of orthodoxy. They proceeded upon the very same premise—the rejection of the Bible as the only absolute and infallible rule of faith—but they attempted to redress their unbelief in such a way that it would be more acceptable to the masses and more orthodox-sounding. The Biblical and orthodox doctrines essential to the faith are just as much repudiated as ever, but the repudiation is couched in such a clever disguise that it often goes unnoticed. Liberalism is not dead! Liberal churchmen have not been converted to the orthodox faith! They have only done what liberals have always prided themselves in being able to do—fit their message to the times. The liberal establishment which spearheads the mad drive for a monstrous world church is no more orthodox now than it has ever been. Through a deceitful game of semantic delusion it is seeking to sell the public a thoroughly heterodox bill of goods. And what is sadly true is that multitudes of laymen are being persuaded to buy the product. Most of them are not aware of the fact that their purchase will ultimately involve the surrender of whatever remains of their church's liberties and will align them, whether they like it or not, with those men and movements which are diametrically opposed to the faith once delivered unto the saints—the faith of our fathers.

Concerned Christians should not be deceived into thinking that the builders of the proposed ecumenical church are without a plan and program. They are by no means without a detailed blueprint by which they propose to reach their goal. Of course, the general public must not know that when the liberal plan is fully realized the present form of church life as to its doctrine, mission and ministry will be completely restructured. Dr. Colin W. Williams, Executive Director of the Department of Evangelism of the National Council of Churches of Christ and Chairman of the Department of Studies in Evangelism of the World Council of Churches, has prepared a brochure entitled, *Where in the World*, which outlines rather clearly the hostility of the ecumenists toward the present form of the local church. The concept of the local church which approves it being centered around the homes of the members who worship in a building dedicated to that purpose and who are shepherded by an ordained minister is considered by Williams as "morphological fundamentalism." The concept of the church as the proclaimer and protector of truth must be replaced by a new concept which puts the church in dialogue with the world. Even more than that, it is contended that "the world should write the agenda" for the church. Such a concept is altogether foreign to the New Testament which calls upon the church to bear a witness to the world which is lost and under the curse of God.

The basic problem of the rejection of the inspiration and authority of the Bible which plagued the founders of liberal theology and was embraced by the attempt of church union from the very beginning still characterizes the present ecumenical leadership. The doctrine that the Bible is the inspired and inerrant Word of God is rejected by them. *Unity Trends*, edited by the Department of Faith and Order of the National Council of Churches in consultation with the Roman Catholic Bishops Committee of Ecumenical and Inter-religious Affairs, published a report which was also accepted by the World Council of Churches' Faith and Order Commission which clearly repudiated the doctrine of the full and final authority of the Bible. The September 15, 1968 issue of *Unity Trends* stated: "The Bible is in many of its parts the product of historical process. It came into being through historical events and experiences and through reflection upon them. Traditions and writings were handed down in Israel and in the Early Church, and were often in the course of long periods combined, reworked and reinterpreted in the light of later historical situations. The Bible contains a collection of very diverse literary traditions, the contents of which often stand in tension with one another." This same document maintains that the Bible contains "unhistorical" and "unauthentic" elements.

This rejection of the historic orthodox position and the witness of the Bible to its own inerrancy and authority has been the background and continues to be the basis of the modern drive for church union.[4]

4See Robert Lightner's *Neo-Liberalism* (Nutley, New Jersey: Craig Press, 1970), for further discussion of the theological background.

III

HISTORICAL LANDMARKS

Factual evidence demonstrates that the rise of theological modernism provided a suitable climate for present-day church unionism. The rejection of the written Word as a completely infallible book and Christ, the living Word, as God manifest in the flesh constitutes a departure from the two most important and impregnable forces of Biblical Christianity. These, along with many related and kindred doctrines, were repudiated by the early enthusiasts of church union. Though the term *Christian* and many other theological terms continued to be used by the modernists, such terms were distorted and invested with new meanings.

The theological liberals or modernists who pioneered the church-union movement did so through the institution and promotion of various organizations. In this chapter these will be discussed in their chronological order. The first to be named was not started by modernists but it included some of them in its membership. This organization needs to be included here because it was the first major attempt at inter-church cooperation and also because eventually those who defected to liberalism withdrew from it and in time proceeded to form their own organizations.

World Evangelical Alliance

Contrary to all the claims and implications which the ecumenists make, Bible-believing Christians were not the ones who originated the divisive spirit and who first separated themselves from others who called themselves Christian. The fact is, disunity, disharmony, and divisiveness in church-union attempts began with those who found themselves in disagreement with the Biblical statement of faith set forth by the World Evangelical Alliance.[5]

Various causes gave rise to the formation of the W.E.A. The ascendency of Roman Catholicism and the apostasy in the Church of England certainly made a contribution to the need for its existence. Also, religious intolerance in many of the European countries as well as denominational fragmentation in the United States lent their support.

A preliminary meeting was held in Liverpool in 1845. Invitations were sent to all parts of the world for Christians to gather in London in August, 1846. Over 800 gathered and accomplished a great deal. A resolution was adopted: "To form a confederation on the basis of great Evangelical principles held in common by them which may afford opportunity to the members of the churches of Christ of cultivating brotherly love, enjoying Christian intercourse, and the promotion of such other objects as they may here after agree to prosecute together; and to form such a confederation under the name of the Evangelical alliance." At the same meeting in 1846 they adopted a statement of principles: "1) The divine inspiration of the Scriptures, their authority and sufficiency. 2) The right and duty of private judgment of the Holy Scriptures. 3) The unity of the Godhead and the Trinity of the persons therein. 4) The utter depravity of human nature in consequence of the fall. 5) The incarnation of the Son of God, His work of atonement for sins, mediatorial intercession and reign. 6) Justification by faith alone. 7) The

---

[5]Hereafter referred to as W.E.A.

work of the Holy Spirit in conversion and sanctification. 8) The immortality of the soul, the resurrection of the body, the judgment of the world by Jesus Christ, the eternal blessedness of the righteous and the eternal punishment of the wicked. 9) The divine institution of the Christian ministry and the obligation and perpetuity of the ordinances of baptism and the Lord's Supper."

From this doctrinal statement it can be seen immediately that the responsible founders of the W.E.A. placed great stress upon the two doctrines in which the liberals were weakest—the doctrines of Scripture and Christ. Soon after the Alliance was formed in England, a similar one arose in the United States as well as in other countries. During the peak of the W.E.A. it made very worthy contributions in behalf of religious liberty, observance of the Lord's Day, temperance, evangelism, and the right of the individual. The concern of the W.E.A. in social matters is seen in the fact that the original constitution forbids membership to slaveholders. A World Day of Prayer and a Universal Week of Prayer were also organized.

Not all the members of the W.E.A. were exempt from the influence of the work of liberal higher criticism and German rationalism which had been so destructively influential in the rise of liberal theology. As the nineteenth century drew to a close certain individuals within the Alliance who had been enamored by liberal theology attempted to adapt the Alliance to fit the liberal structure. However, the strong position which the W.E.A. had taken on the essentials of the Christian faith remained. Those in places of leadership refused to adjust or to soften their position in an effort to have dialogue with men who rejected the inspiration of the Scripture and the deity of Christ. They made it clear to all that as evangelicals they were set not only for the propagation but also for the defense of the gospel.

Being in the minority, the liberals evidently sensed the futility of winning the W.E.A. over to their liberal persuasion and withdrew in 1894. They then organized the Open Church League which became the National Federation of Churches and Christian Workers in 1900. In 1905 this latter organization was replaced by the Federal Council of Churches of Christ in America. As we shall see later, in 1950 the National Council of Churches of

Christ in the U.S.A. replaced the Federal Council of Churches. Liberals were not at all happy with the way in which the W.E.A. was restricted in its membership to evangelicals. They wanted an inclusive federation. Even then they were already ecumenical.

Sadly enough, some of the evangelicals in the W.E.A. also joined the Federal Council of Churches in the naive hope that liberalism was soon to pass away. This action on the part of some evangelicals was at least partially responsible for the demise of the W.E.A. The W.E.A. stands as a historic landmark in the church-union movement because it was a unique attempt at inter-church cooperation and because from it the liberals departed to form organizations which have become milestones toward a one-world church.

Federal Council of Churches of Christ in America

A committee of the liberal oriented National Federation of Churches and Christian Workers called for a conference of the representatives of denominations. From thirty denominations delegates met in New York, November 15-21, 1905. This group mapped out a plan for the formation of the Federal Council of Churches[6] which was ratified in 1908 in Philadelphia.

By comparing the stated purpose and doctrinal basis of the F.C.C. with that of the W.E.A. the wide difference between them becomes immediately apparent. The plan of the F.C.C. centered in the first two of its stated objects: "1) To express the fellowship and catholic unity of the Christian church. 2) To bring the Christian bodies of America into united service for Christ and the world." Here the emphasis was clearly upon the bringing together of all who called themselves Christian. At this point it is well to remember that those who set forth these plans for the F.C.C. were those who withdrew from the W.E.A. because of its Biblical emphasis.

The minimal and undefined doctrinal basis of the F.C.C. provides another striking contrast between the two organizations. The only semblance of a doctrinal statement for the F.C.C. was in its preamble where Jesus Christ is recognized as "divine Lord

---

6Hereafter referred to as F.C.C.

and Saviour." Even the word *divine* was not in the original draft of the preamble until some suggested that it should be to insure the evangelical character of the Council. The insertion of the word *divine* of course by no means made the F.C.C. an evangelical organization. Already at that early date words such as the word *divine* no longer meant what they originally and traditionally meant in orthodox circles. Since the mass of Bible-believers were not yet aware of the liberals' tricks of using orthodox-sounding words and investing them with new meaning, many people were deceived. To the liberals "divine" did not mean "deity." They meant by the term that Christ was simply more divine than man was. It did not distinguish Him in kind from the rest of mankind but only in degree. The late Harry Emerson Fosdick who was praised by the F.C.C. and was one of its preachers put it bluntly: "Of course the divinity of Jesus differs from ours in a degree but not in kind. . . . I think God was in my mother, the source of the loveliness that blessed us there!" Liberals of that day, and this, affirm that Christ is not very God of very God. They merely accept the "divinity" of Christ as an experience out of which an idea grew as men experienced a relatedness to God. They by no means accepted the Biblical portraits and propositional statements about Christ as fixed truth. As one of them said long ago, belief in Christ as Son of God " . . . does not mean that Jesus was God. It means that His life was so filled with the character and power of God that when men have seen Him, they have seen the Father."

The F.C.C. never defined its terms used in the preamble. Inclusion of the Universalists, who candidly deny the deity of Christ, into the F.C.C. in 1946 was further proof that the evangelical-sounding words of the preamble were nothing but a meaningless semantic delusion. Failure of the F.C.C. to define its terms, acceptance of denominations which did not accept the deity of Christ, elevation to leadership in the F.C.C. of those who categorically denied the deity of Christ, and the inability of the F.C.C. to interfere in the doctrinal beliefs of its members because of the lack of its own doctrinal basis and any means of protection against false doctrine, all demonstrate the meaninglessness of the words of its preamble.

Even the secular press recognized the attempts and effects of the F.C.C.'s work. *Newsweek* spoke of the F.C.C. as "a virtual monopoly" in American Protestantism. The attempt and partial success of the F.C.C. in the area of religious radio broadcasting is a case in point. Virtually controlling religious broadcasting time by claiming to represent Protestantism, the F.C.C. utilized almost all the available time for religious broadcasts allotted by the radio network.

Contrary to all its claims such monopolizing efforts of the F.C.C. made it the beginning of the drive for a world church—a historic landmark on the road to church union. The F.C.C. was the fulfillment of Washington Gladden's dream for an organization through which churches could unite for political and social action.

World Council of Churches

A great step was taken in the church-union movement in 1948 in Amsterdam with the formation of the World Council of Churches.[7] Three hundred fifty-two delegates representing 135 denominational bodies met in an assembly and formed the W.C.C. Now representing a constituency of approximately 315 million in all parts of the world, the W.C.C. is a colossal church power second only to the Roman Catholic church in size and influence but virtually identical to it in the way its leaders manage the organizational machinery.

The W.C.C. had its beginnings in a number of other organizations—the Conference on Faith and Order, the Council on Life and Work, and the International Missionary Movement. Each of these was staffed by theological liberals. A committee to begin an "ecumenical movement was called for in 1936 by the Life and Work and the Faith and Order Movements. Already in 1937 this committee recommended that these Movements seek for the formation of the W.C.C. In 1938 the International Missionary Council joined in the attempt. The outbreak of World War II delayed the plans. After the war in 1946 at Geneva, Switzerland final steps were taken. At Amsterdam, Holland on August 23,

---

[7]Hereafter referred to as W.C.C. For a list of constituency see Appendix A.

1948, with the head of the State Church of England as chairman of the committee, the W.C.C. came into existence.

From its very inception the W.C.C., like the F.C.C., had an extremely brief and variously interpreted doctrinal basis. This was no doubt intentional. The W.C.C.'s Basis states, " The World Council of Churches is a fellowship of churches which accept our Lord Jesus Christ as God and Savior according to the Scriptures and therefore seek to fulfill together their common calling to the glory of the one God, Father, Son and Holy Spirit."[8] Since the W.C.C. does not concern itself as to how the churches interpret this, it therefore really has no doctrinal statement at all. Lucas Vischer, Director of the Department on Faith and Order of the W.C.C. made this clear in the April, 1968 *United Church Herald*. He said, "Therefore, must not the church itself—when it formulates the Gospel—remain open for new insights? Must it not in the last analysis attribute a provisional character to all of its affirmations and confessions?" Without a standard interpretation there can be no standard meaning. Like the F.C.C. the wide variety of doctrinal beliefs of member churches clearly indicates the lack of any attempt on the part of the W.C.C. to be orthodox in doctrine. Even a casual reading of the articles and books written by the leaders of the W.C.C. from its beginning to the present hour reveals the rejection of the inspiration and absolute authority of the Bible, the complete deity of Christ and many other essentials of the Christian faith. Even one of the W.C.C. presidents said recently, " . . . there is much disagreement in the W.C.C. as to who Jesus Christ is, where he is found and how he is identified" (Religious News Service report from Canterbury, England, August 18, 1969). The admission of the Hicksite Quakers, a sect which denies the deity of Christ, into the membership of the W.C.C. further solidifies the fact that the brief doctrinal statement of the W.C.C. is meaningless.

Conflicting statements from W.C.C. leaders present a cloudy picture regarding the purposes and trends of the W.C.C. to become a sort of superchurch. When W. A. Visser 't Hooft was the General Secretary, he denied any such intentions. In the early

---

[8]*Questions and Answers about the World Council of Churches,* World Council of Churches, New York.

days of the W.C.C. others made similar disavowals. Yet it is strange, on the other hand, to hear Samuel McCrea Cavert, who was the Secretary of the F.C.C. and the Executive Secretary of the W.C.C. from 1953 to 1957, say, "We should not conclude that because the churches have not delegated any authority to the Council at the beginning, they will never be willing to do so. It is entirely possible that if the sense of need for a more united church increases and if the Council commends itself strongly to the churches by the way it fulfills its present limited functions, the time may come when the churches will desire to assign certain responsibilities to it and to confer on it a constitutional authority in certain specified matters."9 More will be said in another chapter on the one-church goal of the ecumenical leaders. We merely want to establish at this point the link between the liberal oriented W.C.C. and the present drive for church union. From the W.C.C.'s very beginning the leaders of the organization have, through many books and articles published at the time of its formation and since, indicated the connection between the W.C.C. and a united church.

Though attempts at denial are frequently made by W.C.C. leaders, it is an established fact that international communism is at work in and through the W.C.C. Joseph Hromadka, the official representative of the Evangelical Church of the Czech Brethren who attended the Amsterdam assembly of the W.C.C., was an admitted communist. Other communists were present at the Amsterdam organizational meeting as well. T. C. Chao of Red China was elected as one of the presidents of the W.C.C. in the concluding plenary sessions. Beyond its ecumenical emphasis the chief concern of the W.C.C. is sociopolitical. Practically all of its policy statements deal with social and political matters. There is much discussion about communism, socialism, capitalism, the United Nations, peaceful coexistence and atomic warfare. The 1954 Evanston, Illinois meeting of the W.C.C. revealed glaring conflicts on its theme, "Christ the Hope of the World." There was hopeless confusion as to who Christ was and what kind of hope He brought for the world. Shifting the discussion to social

---

9*The Universal Church in God's Design,* of The Amsterdam Assembly Series (New York: Harper Brothers, 1949) , p. 199.

action saved the day at Evanston, and ever since that emphasis has been a chief concern of the W.C.C. Strong antagonism against capitalism and friendly regard for communism has been characteristic of the W.C.C.

In New Delhi, India, in 1961 the W.C.C. demonstrated beyond question its sympathies toward atheistic communism. There it received into its membership the Russian Orthodox Church along with several other churches from behind the Iron Curtain. Only the underground church remains free from communist jurisdiction. The communist-controlled Russian Church was invited originally to the 1948 Amsterdam meeting. It refused to come because it viewed the W.C.C. as a rival to the communist conspiracy. No doubt Eugene Carson Blake and nine others were responsible for allaying these fears by their visit to Russia in 1956. Certainly the Evanston assembly of the W.C.C. and its declaration on world peace and disarmament appealed to the sixteen-member delegation of communists, headed by Archbishop Nikodim, and paved the way for the acceptance of the Russian Orthodox Church in 1961. The Archbishop who now directs the affairs of the Russians in the W.C.C. is an avowed communist. He collaborates with Soviet authorities to keep the church in Russia under government control.

The fourth and most recent assembly of the W.C.C., held in Uppsala, Sweden on July 18, 1969, provided more evidence for the W.C.C.'s communist sympathies. Six prominent church leaders were elected to serve as the W.C.C.'s presidents until the next assembly to be held in six or seven years. Among these six was Patriarch German, head of the Serbian Orthodox Church of Yugoslavia. Even the Serbian Orthodox Church in the United States recognizes him as a communist agent and refuses to serve under him.

The constant and repeated attempts of the W.C.C. to pressure for the acceptance of Communist China into the United Nations is another proof of its interest in atheistic communism. The W.C.C. organized the World Conference on Church and Society which was held in Geneva, Switzerland in 1966. At this conference Communist China was praised as "Saviour" and there was open support of Christian violence to effect social changes.

Also, Herbert A. Philbrick, nine years an undercover agent for the F.B.I., reported in the April, 1966 *Dollar Hollar* that the communists in clerical garb were scheming behind the scenes to foist a "marxist" propaganda line on the W.C.C. at their scheduled meeting in Geneva in July, 1966. They thought it would be an opportune time since the theme of the W.C.C. for that meeting was to be "Church and Society."

Everyone knows of course that the W.C.C. is broad enough to include virtually any theological position. The Uppsala meeting of the W.C.C. was labeled by the secular press as the most widely representative meeting in the history of the ecumenical movement. Reporting in prospect on the meeting the *National Catholic Reporter* of June 26, 1968 said that "every theological position will be represented at this assembly from the death of God school to the reformulators and traditionalists." It should be noted too in retrospect that the representations did not stop with theological positions. In addition to the broad spectrum of theologies present the W.C.C.'s twentieth anniversary meeting in Uppsala also revealed the Council's view on a number of other crucial issues. Condoning and welcoming communism, sanctioning and promoting violence, added to a frantic drive for the formation of a worldwide "Christian" community were not enough for the W.C.C. leaders. Christians who were shocked by the film "The Parable" shown at the Protestant Pavilion of the New York World's Fair in which Christ was presented as a clown would be completely aghast at the latest of such films. A new film prepared under church auspices for the W.C.C. assembly in Uppsala was entitled "Another Pilgrim." The film centers in a traditional worship service. At the end the minister removes his clothes to symbolize the stripping away of barriers between people. The W.C.C. says it depicts "in poetic form the exhilaration of modern man, as well as his bewilderment in a world where the only permanent factor is change."

The W.C.C.'s softness and sympathy toward atheistic communism and its endorsement of violent revolution has found most recent expression in the decision of the Council in September, 1970 to allocate $200,000 to what it calls "anti-racist" organizations. These "anti-racist" organizations are the anti-government guerrilla groups in South Africa which are opposed to South Africa's racial policies. Little wonder that the Johannesburg *Star* raised the question, "What in God's name does the World Council of Churches think it is doing?"

That which is causing so much division and even threats within the W.C.C. over this action is that much of the money will go to black African liberation movements, some of which are definitely supported by the communists. These organizations are involved in various stages of violent revolution against minority groups in South Africa, Rhodesia, and Portuguese colonies. Another complaint is that the Executive Council did not consult, as is often the case, the constituent members before appropriating the money. Furthermore, the $200,000 gift is to be followed by considerably more.

This action by the W.C.C. Executive Committee has been criticized by many. South African Prime Minister B. J. Vorster even urged South African churches to reconsider their relationship to the W.C.C. because of this grant. Robert Selby Taylor, Anglican Archbishop, said he was "almost certain" some churches would withdraw from the W.C.C. because of the action. According to a Religious News Service report, the United Evangelical Lutheran Church in Germany decided not to support the W.C.C.'s program to combat racism.

In spite of all the verbal protest, Eugene Carson Blake, Secretary General of the W.C.C., reportedly told representatives of the Evangelical Church in Germany that the grants will be carried out even without total support of the W.C.C.'s constituency.

Much more could be said about the W.C.C. Enough has been presented to demonstrate the eligibility of this global organization to rank as an historic landmark toward church union.

National Council of Churches of Christ in the U.S.A.

What the W.C.C. represents internationally the National Council of Churches[10] represents nationally. Only a brief treatment will therefore be necessary here. The Council was born out of the F.C.C. and eleven other interdenominational agencies in

---

[10]Hereafter referred to as N.C.C. For list of constituency see Appendix B.

1950. Today it claims to represent thirty-three denominations with a total membership of about 42 million persons. The N.C.C. is governed by the General Assembly which meets every three years. A General Board of approximately 250 members elected by the General Assembly from its own membership governs the Council between the meetings. A General Secretary is responsible for recommending and implementing policies and programs of the Council. Finances for the N.C.C.'s program are drawn largely from the membership. Denominations affiliated with the N.C.C. give a percentage of the income from their local churches to the N.C.C. These funds, and others which the N.C.C. receives, provide the basis for meeting their annual budget which currently reaches nearly $20 million.

David Emerson Gumaer, contributing editor to *The Review of the News* and formerly an undercover agent for the Chicago Police Intelligence in connection with the youth apparatus of the Communist Party, summarized the N.C.C.'s financial program this way: "The program is of such magnitude that in 1968, alone, the National Council of Churches expended over $19 million on a worldwide network of Leftist projects. In that year, however, the N.C.C. *collected* $24,819,000 from gullible American Christians and tax-exempt Leftist foundations."[11]

The minimal doctrinal statement of the N.C.C. has never been defined and is even less satisfactory than that of the W.C.C. The single item in the constitution of the N.C.C. which is supposed to reveal the doctrinal belief of the Council and its members is belief in "Jesus Christ as divine Lord and Saviour." Refusal of the N.C.C. to make any commitment regarding the Bible or to speak of Christ as God and Savior reveals the intent of such a minimal statement. Also, a casual glance at the list of member churches will reveal the lack of any adherence to doctrinal orthodoxy on the part of a number of the members. The type of leadership the N.C.C. has and continues to choose also reveals its unorthodox theological position. From the earliest years to the present, avowed and well-known deniers of the historic Christian faith have held key positions of leadership. Add to this the evi-

---

11*American Opinion*, February, 1970, p. 49.

dence of the N.C.C.'s theologically liberal persuasion seen in its publications and those of its leaders and the case is proven beyond question. This is not to say there are no evangelicals supposedly represented by the N.C.C. It is to say though that the official position of the N.C.C. and the position of its leadership is avowedly liberal.

The General Board of the N.C.C. met in advance of the Council's annual week-long convention in 1966 and not only adopted a resolution calling for the end of the military draft but also adopted another resolution recognizing the Roman Catholic Church as being in agreement with the preamble to the Council's constitution.

In the same year the N.C.C. accepted into its membership the Church of the New Jerusalem. This church candidly rejects the doctrines of the Trinity, the deity, substitutionary atonement, and the bodily resurrection of Christ in keeping with the views of its founder, Emmanuel Swedenberg.

As recently as January, 1970 the Reorganized Church of Jesus Christ of Latter-Day Saints (Mormon) won recognition of its eligibility for membership in the N.C.C. Even though this Reorganized Church is by far smaller than the Salt Lake City group, yet it is the second largest Mormon body, and its recognition by the N.C.C. illustrates the woefully weak doctrinal position of the Council. Though this recognition does not mean the same as membership, it does mean that the group can now participate in the work of N.C.C. agencies.

From the very beginning the N.C.C. has aided and curried the favor of the communist cause. Reflecting the changeover from the F.C.C. to the N.C.C. in Cleveland in 1950 and the carry-over of communist affiliations to the N.C.C., J. B. Matthews who compiled *Appendix IX* of the Dies Committee on Un-American Activities said, "In the formal constitution of the National Council of Churches in Cleveland, one representative from each of the participating denominations signed the official book which became the Document of Record. Eleven of these 29 signers of the official book have public records of affiliation with pro-communist enterprises. . . . There were 358 clergymen who were voting delegates to the constituting convention. . . . Of these clergymen, 123 (or 34 percent) have had affiliations with Communist projects and enterprises. That represents a high degree of Communist penetration."[12]

For years communist publications such as the *Worker* have praised actions and activities of the N.C.C. because many of the plans and programs of the communist world and those of the N.C.C. overlap and are identical. The first woman president of the N.C.C., Dr. Cynthia Wedel, elected at the Council's December, 1969 meeting, is said by *The New York Times* to occupy the "highest symbolic post in American Protestantism." *The Times* also revealed that Dr. Wedel is the Associate Director of what has been called the "wildly Leftist Center for Voluntarism in the Institute for Applied Behavioral Science in Washington."[13]

The N.C.C. has repeatedly castigated the United States and has sided with Russia on numerous political matters. On more than one occasion the Council has advocated socialism, federal aid to education, and the welfare state. It has opposed states' rights and often encouraged racial strife. The key assistance given to the N.C.C. to carry out its work in the social-political areas has been its political lobbies in Washington and many state capitals. A published list of thirty-two Policy Statements of the N.C.C. through 1965 reveals that only seven of them had anything whatsoever to do with religious matters. All the others were sociopolitical in nature.

This kind of emphasis follows a carefully outlined plan. It is no surprise, to many who are informed, to learn that the means by which the N.C.C. makes itself known and pressures state and federal governments for its goals is to purport to speak for the entire church. Already the makings of a superchurch are in process. And the more N.C.C. leaders disavow any intention of building a superchurch the more untruthful their claims become as the facts are faced squarely. The formation of the N.C.C. marked a giant stride toward the death of free, sovereign and autonomous local churches. Through it there is in process a massive modernistic machinery determined eventually to control all local church bodies. Already, millions of people are a part of

12*Ibid.*, p. 59.
13*Ibid.*, p. 67.

and lend their support to an organization which has spelled the doom on the action of their church's desire and decision regarding education, missions, social welfare, the distribution of at least part of their monies and many, many other areas of church life.

Wise to the effect any claim of building a superchurch would have upon evangelicals within their movement, leaders of the N.C.C. vigorously deny any such intent. First, there must be the conditioning work of brainwashing. A primary effort in this direction is to alter the thinking of the public regarding the structure and traditional view concerning the essence and ministry of a church. Only the conservative element in the N.C.C. would pose any possible threat to the N.C.C. goals. Liberal church members, which constitute the majority of its constituents, could not care less if a superchurch comes into existence. In fact, many of them think it would be the greatest thing which could ever happen to the churches.

Reams of political releases have been and still are being released to the American public through all the modern means of mass media. It is always made clear that these decisions represent the voice of multiplied millions of American churchmen. The fact of the matter is that by far most of the same multiplied millions were never consulted about their views. When the truth is known, most of the ways by which the N.C.C. exerts itself and makes its influence known are apart from the ordinary processes whereby constituent members are given an opportunity to voice their opinion. The N.C.C. performs now as a superchurch. Often through one department of the N.C.C. appeal is made to its members to take certain actions. Such appeals frequently are not the voice of the appointed leaders of member denominations at all but simply the idea and work of one or a few pawned off on the American public as the voice of the N.C.C. membership. In spite of its claim to speak *to* the churches rather than *for* the churches it usually does the exact opposite. Executives and staff members at the head office of the N.C.C., located at 475 Riverside Drive, New York, send out much material designed to influence the thinking and actions of Christians. Messages are sent out which are read in many pulpits to influence millions of people. These are not the work of the representatives but of the upper echelon only. The same is true of the many articles on such things as church-state problems, immigration laws of the United States, medical care, and the rights of minority groups, etc. Even the study books and films are prepared by only a few who pretend to speak for the total constituency of the N.C.C.

Both friend and foe of the N.C.C. would have to agree on one basic fact—the N.C.C. has been and is today a great landmark toward church union.

Consultation on Church Union

Those pushing for church union acknowledge that a "fresh attempt at church union was precipitated" on December 4, 1960. Interestingly enough, the occasion was the triannual meeting of the N.C.C. On that date Eugene Carson Blake, Stated Clerk of the United Presbyterian Church in the U.S.A., preached a sermon entitled, "A Proposal Toward the Reunion of Christ's Church." He delivered the sermon in the Grace (Episcopal) Cathedral of San Francisco, California which was then pastored by Bishop James A. Pike. In the sermon he said, "Led, I pray by the Holy Spirit, I propose to the Protestant Episcopal Church that it together with the United Presbyterian Church in the United States of America invite the Methodist Church and the United Church of Christ to form with us a plan of church union both catholic and reformed on the basis of the principles I shall later in this sermon suggest. Any other churches which find that they can accept both the principles and plan would also be warmly invited to unite with us."

On the basis of this proposal the four above named denominations were represented in the first official meeting on April 9 and 10, 1962 in Washington, D.C. "to enter into the exploration of the establishment of a united church." Thus the Council on Church Union[14] was born. Since that time much progress has been made toward the intended goal of "the establishment of a united church." Already in 1962 at the Washington, D.C. meeting the Disciples of Christ and the Evangelical United Brethren

---

[14]Hereafter referred to as C.O.C.U. For a list of members see Appendix C.

were invited to join the Consultation. These two denominations already had existing union conversations with, respectively, the United Church of Christ and the Methodist Church. Both the Disciples of Christ and the Evangelical United Brethren Church accepted the invitation. An executive committee and secretary were elected, and March, 1963 was set as the date for the next C.O.C.U. meeting to be convened at Oberlin, Ohio. At this second plenary meeting consensus was reached on the C.O.C.U.'s view of Scripture and tradition and the relation of these to each other. More will be said later regarding the C.O.C.U.'s view of Scripture and other key doctrines. At the third plenary meeting in Princeton, New Jersey on April 13-16, 1964 consensus was reached concerning the ordinances of the church. On April 4-8, 1965 in Lexington, Kentucky the African Episcopal Church became the seventh member of C.O.C.U. Also, at this same plenary meeting, consensus was reached on ministry. Dallas, Texas was the place for the fifth plenary meeting on May 2-5, 1966. In the same meeting where there was approval of *Principles of Church Union* the Presbyterian Church in the United States and the African Methodist Episcopal Church Zion became the eighth and ninth participating members. The sixth plenary meeting of C.O.C.U. was held in Cambridge, Massachusetts, May 1-4, 1967. At that time approval was given to *Guidelines for the Structure of the Church,* and there was a decision to begin to develop a plan of union. In January of 1967 the C.O.C.U. received a tenth church—Christian Methodist Episcopal Church. March 25-28, 1968 was scheduled for the seventh plenary meeting. During that time in Dayton, Ohio a *Provisional Structure of the United Church* was adopted. Also, by the time of that meeting the Methodist Church had merged with the Evangelical United Brethren Church to form the United Methodist Church. This reduced the members of the C.O.C.U. to nine. A commission was appointed in Dayton to prepare the draft of a plan of union. The eighth plenary meeting of C.O.C.U. was held in Atlanta, Georgia, March 17-20, 1969. The delegates were given a "Preliminary Outline for a Plan of Union" and also "Guidelines for Local Interchurch Action" for their churches to study. A poll was conducted of the C.O.C.U. delegates for a proposed name for the coming united church. It was decided that the 1970 meeting would be held in St. Louis, Missouri, March 9-13.

Perhaps one of the most significant things about the 1969 Atlanta meeting was the large number of observer-consultant churches represented. This representation included the following: American Baptist Convention, Anglican Church of Canada, Anglican-Methodist Conversations in the West Indies, Christian Church in Canada, Church of the Brethren, Council of Community Churches, Cumberland Presbyterian Church, Evangelische Kirche der Union, Lutheran Council of the United States of America, Moravian Church in America—Northern Province, Reformed Church in America, Religious Society of Friends Philadelphia Yearly Meeting, Roman Catholic Church, Standing Conference of the Canonical Orthodox Bishops in the Americas, United Church of Canada, National Council of Churches, World Council of Churches.

In preparation for each plenary session of C.O.C.U. there are twelve commissions or committees. These work behind the scenes and prepare papers and reports for the delegates to adopt at the meetings. The delegates of the C.O.C.U. represent, at least statistically, some 25 million church members. No doubt, multitudes of these are deceived by the terminology used by the C.O.C.U. spokesmen. The phrase which constantly appears in connection with C.O.C.U. is that it seeks a church that is truly catholic, truly evangelical, and truly reformed. Upon examination of the meaning of these words as they are used by the C.O.C.U., their meaninglessness becomes apparent. The word *catholic* implies whole or universal, thus reference is made to the entire church—the totality of professing Christendom. When used by the C.O.C.U. in reference to its future church, this word is meant to imply that the C.O.C.U. church, whatever it may be called, will have the proper balance, emphasis and combination of all that may be called Christian. It will be all-inclusive. The greatest semantic delusion in this orthodox-sounding phrase of C.O.C.U. is the word *evangelical*. This appears, on the surface, to say that the C.O.C.U. doctrine and ambition is thoroughly orthodox. To the great masses of Christians the word *evangelical* means the same as *Biblical, true,* or *orthodox* as opposed to *un-*

biblical, false, or *unorthodox.* C.O.C.U. leaders do not mean, by using the term *evangelical,* what that word normally connotes when used in reference, for example, to evangelicals as opposed to liberals. One wonders though whether the C.O.C.U. has not intentionally used the word so that it can hide behind the impression it creates and, the meaning it sustains in the minds of the masses. As used by C.O.C.U., "Evangelical suggests reliance upon the saving and redeeming power of Christ and upon the Scriptures. . . . " As shall be demonstrated, the doctrinal beliefs set forth by the C.O.C.U. from its very beginning, especially those related to the Christ of Scripture and Christ's Scripture, belie even this meaning in the word. The final word in the C.O.C.U. motto is the word *reformed.* In 1967 the following meaning was given to this word by C.O.C.U.: " 'Reformed,' perhaps better 'reforming,' suggests a church constantly under the corrective guidance of the Holy Spirit, constantly renewed, reviewed and reconstructed so as to be pure and serviceable for its day." When these three words, *catholic, evangelical,* and *reformed,* especially the latter two, appear without any explanation, as they generally do, an entirely false impression of the nature of the C.O.C.U. is created.

A perusal of the writings of C.O.C.U. leaders and of C.O.C.U. publications reveals the anti-biblical views of this gigantic attempt to build a superchurch. Eugene Carson Blake's initial sermon proposing the C.O.C.U. made very clear his view of the Scriptures. He said, "So long as the wording 'sola scriptura' is required, no bridge can be made between catholic and evangelical." He went on to say that Protestants have now "come to recognize the right place of tradition. . . . " In that same famous sermon he said, "Finally the reunited church must find the way to include within its catholicity (and because of it) a wide diversity of theological formulation of the faith and a variety of worship and liturgy including worship that is non-liturgical." The official statement of the C.O.C.U. on the Scriptures reveals its terribly weak and deceptive view. That statement says: "The united church acknowledges that the Holy Scriptures of the Old and New Testaments have a unique authority. They witness to God's revelation fulfilled in Jesus Christ. . . . They are the inspired writings which bear witness to the divine deeds in our history. . . . " C.O.C.U. also stresses the fact that "the Bible must . . . become God's living Word to us." While such statements may succeed in deceiving many, they by no means square with the Bible's testimony to itself or with the historic view of the church. The Bible is God's revelation to man. It is the Word of God apart from any reception or response on the part of man. Whether man receives it or not, the Word of God stands written and forever settled in Heaven. ·

Such a weak view of Scripture very logically creates false views on other doctrines contained in its pages. On the matter of salvation, for example, C.O.C.U. believes that " . . . through baptism (water) God engrafts the individual person into his people as a living member of the body of Christ." Both baptism and communion are viewed as means of grace by the C.O.C.U. Evidently the leadership of C.O.C.U. believes that all men will eventually be saved—no one will be forever lost in Hell. Frequently, they speak of the salvation for the whole of mankind. Peter Day, a delegate to C.O.C.U. and one thoroughly involved in the ecumenical movement, presented the C.O.C.U. philosophy of universalism (all will be saved) when he said: "In its deepest sense, the task of the ecumenical movement is not to unite churches, but to unite mankind in the body of Christ. . . . It is far more important—and, in the deepest sense, more ecumenical —to give a cup of cold water to one of Christ's little ones than to read a book about Methodism or visit the local Presbyterian church. It is more ecumenical, because it has a more powerful bearing on the question of making mankind one in Christ."[15]

That C.O.C.U. continues to exist as a landmark toward eventual church union is a fact beyond question. Robert Hednut a spokesman and enthusiast for C.O.C.U., put it in words beyond dispute when he wrote in *Presbyterian Life*: "The Consultation on Church Union is nothing more or less than a power grab. As such, I applaud it. For years the Protestant church has been naive when it comes to power. We have spiritual power. Yes, but when it comes to temporal power, we are not bright.

---

[15]Peter Day, *Tomorrow's Church: Catholic, Evangelical, Reformed* (New York: The Seabury Press, 1969), pp. 18, 19.

We can convert people, but we have a hard time moving them. We can change them, but we have a hard time getting them to change society. The *laissez-faire* ball game is over. That is what the Consultation on Church Union is saying. We have big business and we have big government, and now we need a big church. We need nine denominations and 25,000,000 people joined together to do what none of them can do alone. We had big business and we had big government because they work. Now we need a big church because it can work too."

What Next?

Careful study of the historic landmarks toward church union reviewed thus far raises the very logical question, What will the next move be? Several factors have raised this question in the minds of many—even among some within the church-union movement.

There seems to be indication that both the N.C.C. and the W.C.C. need to be supplanted by a new organization. At least it is becoming evident to ecumenists that these councils must be thoroughly revamped. One of the major reasons behind this thinking stems from the growing rapprochement between Roman Catholics and Protestants. Recently a meeting between Pope Paul VI and half a dozen leading American Protestants in Rome accelerated the idea. Then the creation of a fourteen-member committee to study Roman Catholic membership in the N.C.C. also furthered the concept. Perhaps the most obvious evidence for such a drive was the proposal from a high-ranking Lutheran leader that the N.C.C. be phased out in favor of a more inclusive organization. What this all amounts to is that, for many, the N.C.C. has accomplished its purpose and there is need to move on to greater accomplishments toward church union.

The December, 1969 N.C.C.'s eighth triennial meeting brought closer to reality the proposal mentioned above. At that meeting of the N.C.C. General Assembly the General Secretary, R. H. Edwin Espy, called for the creation of a "more representative" body. He said the "new 'General Ecumenical Council' could function as an organizational umbrella for a large variety of interdenominational agencies. . . . " This, Espy explained, would embrace "Roman Catholics, Pentecostals, and other Christians who are not now among its 33 Protestant and Orthodox member churches" (*Newsweek*, December 15, 1969, p. 97). Many N.C.C. leaders acknowledge that the N.C.C. is in serious trouble, particularly financial, and is in need of an overhaul. In some cases member churches failed to provide support for the many so-called priority programs on race and peace thus jeopardizing and curtailing the N.C.C.'s program. To implement the desires for a "General Ecumenical Council" a fifteen-member ecumenical task force was created in January, 1970 in Tulsa, Oklahoma, in the longest General Board meeting in its history, to move ahead with restructuring the N.C.C. The General Secretary, Espy, and the new President, Dr. Wedel, appointed the task force.

Search for a new organization to replace the N.C.C. continues. In June, 1970 leaders of the N.C.C. met in Washington, D.C., to, as Louis Cassels put it, "consider how the gravely ailing National Council of Churches (N.C.C.) may be replaced or resuscitated." Though the N.C.C.'s denominational representatives are not sure at this time what will become of the N.C.C. or which direction it will take, there is consensus of opinion that it will certainly not become orthodox. No doubt, the N.C.C.'s biggest problem and hindrance to the accomplishments of its goals has been and is now a financial one.

Four options have been presented to the N.C.C. by its own leaders for change. Some feel a simple revamping of the Council giving more power to the governing General Board would solve most of its problems. Others think the N.C.C. should be broadened into a more general ecumenical fellowship which would include and involve the Roman Catholic Church and many evangelical Protestant bodies not now in the N.C.C. In fact, Dr. David Hunter, the N.C.C. Deputy General Secretary, discussed such action at a press conference. Plans are to invite groups not associated with the N.C.C. to a gathering where the restructure of the N.C.C. will be discussed. Still other ecumenists are convinced the N.C.C. must be scrapped and replaced by a new organization to be called "Churches United for Social Justice."

This new organization would concentrate all its attention on social action programs.

The chief concern of N.C.C. leaders seems to be with those groups outside of it. Of special concern are large groups such as the Southern Baptist Convention and the Missouri Lutheran Synod. Whatever form the new structure will take, it will undoubtedly be designed to include Rome and as many conservative Protestant groups as possible. In September, 1970 at Phoenix, Arizona a task force was appointed by the N.C.C. to come up with a plan which would accomplish this goal.

That task force presented a plan of restructure to the General Board in January, 1971. In brief, the plan called for a decentralized structure which would require denominational support for the N.C.C. programs before they were enacted. The plan was an attempt at least to avoid the criticism usually leveled, and rightly so, against the N.C.C.'s General Board for purporting to speak for its 42.5 million churchgoers often without ever consulting them. The General Board refused the task force's desire that the new plan be presented to member denominations for approval. Instead, a new committee was appointed to revise the plan before giving it serious consideration. The basic reason, it seems, for the General Board's refusal of the task-force plan was its fear of the repercussion from the N.C.C.'s militant black constituency. As activist Methodist Bishop James Matthews said, "This model might make the wrong people happy." The new committee is to present its report at a meeting of the General Board scheduled for September, 1971 in New Orleans.

Responsible and informed evangelicals believe that very likely the Roman Catholic Church will soon become a part of an organization, whatever it will be called, which will of course include Protestants but which will have been set up by Roman Catholics. If and when such a conciliar realignment becomes a reality or a General Ecumenical Council is born, it will probably not affect the C.O.C.U. The N.C.C. and C.O.C.U. are not organically related at the present time. It is no secret that the C.O.C.U. has stolen the stage, at least for a time and in many respects, from the N.C.C.

On May 9-13, 1970 in St. Louis at the annual meeting of

C.O.C.U. a draft document developed by a commision of C.O.C.U. was presented. The Plan of Union outlined in the draft presents the proposed name for the 25 million-member church which is to result from the merger as the "Church of Christ Uniting." This name will allow the ecumenists to continue to use the same C.O.C.U. label as had been used in the consultation stages. The Plan also states that the proposed church would "seek communion with other churches in the U.S. and world." The plan was adopted and has gone to the nine denominations which are a part of C.O.C.U. for further study and eventual "irrevocable commitment" to it. This Plan represents the foundation, the substructure, of the proposed one holy catholic visible church on earth.[16]

There are two basic questions which every believer must ask with reference to the Plan: (1) What is the theological, doctrinal platform adopted by the Plan? and (2) How will the local churches which are a part of the new Church of Christ Uniting be run?

In answer to the first question it must be said that nowhere in the Plan of Union published by the C.O.C.U. is there any definition of what the envisioned church believes on specific doctrines such as the Person and work of Christ, the Person and work of the Holy Spirit, man, sin, Satan, the church, or last things. The Plan of Union does include a chapter entitled "The Living Faith." In this section the theological basis of the proposed church is stated: "The faith of the united church is expressed in Scripture, Tradition, creeds, confessions, preaching, liturgies and the Lord's Supper and in action in obedience to our Lord."[17]

What the designers of the C.O.C.U. mean by the minimal doctrinal statements is most important. Scripture is said to be of "unique and *normative* authority." "The Scripture *witnesses* to God's revelation, fulfilled in Christ, and to man's response to that revelation. . . . It *testifies* to God's mighty acts of creation

---

16Two excellent articles by Dr. Harold Lindsell presenting a critique of this Plan of Union appeared in *Christianity Today*, October 9, 1970 and October 23, 1970.

17*A Plan of Union for the Church of Christ Uniting*, Executive Committee of the Consultation on Church Union, Princeton, New Jersey, 1970, p. 25.

and re-creation . . . . " The books of the Apocrypha "may also be used as part of the *edifying* literature of the people of God."[18]

The proposed church accepts the Apostles' and Nicene Creeds "as witnesses of Tradition to the mighty acts of God in Scripture." Added to these two historic creeds the new church will also accept the Covenants and Confession of its member churches. The Plan of Union makes it very clear that none of the bases of authority—Scripture, Tradition, Creeds or Covenants, and Confessions of the churches—will be binding upon anyone in the new church. The Church of Christ Uniting "will not use any of these Confessions as the exclusive requirement for all, nor permit them to become a basis for divisions in the new community."[19] Such a statement agrees with an earlier one in the Plan to the effect that Scripture is to be "interpreted in the light of the Tradition."[20]

Careful examination of the proposed Plan of Union makes it immediately apparent that the framers of the Plan had no intention of embracing the historic orthodox and Biblical view of the total, absolute, and exclusive authority of the Bible. Throughout the Plan, orthodox-sounding words appear, but they are invested with new and foreign meanings.

The second basic query, "How will the local churches which are a part of the new church be run?" can easily be answered. The new United Church will accept the "historic episcopate." This means the church will have bishops who will act as "guardians of worship and sacraments." They will also have power to appoint ministers. All the local churches which are a part of the denominations planning to merge will be organized into "Parishes." The legal control of all property, the power to elect officers to govern the local assemblies will be under the control of these "Parishes." In brief, may it be said, the type of church government proposed for the new church spells the end of any type of congregational control. Harold Lindsell summarized the new church's type of government very well when he said, "For those who believe in the tradition of the historic episcopate, much will be gained, nothing lost. For those who believe in other

---

18*Ibid.*
19*Ibid.*, p. 27.
20*Ibid.*, p. 26.

polities the Union will mean that they lose their unique identities" (*Christianity Today,* October 23, 1970, p. 10).

Even those not Biblically oriented and without any theological ax to grind have observed the anemic doctrinal basis of the new church. *Time* magazine gave this report of the Plan: "The plan's references to doctrine and scripture are intentionally, and perhaps sensibly, ambiguous. The church 'accepts the Apostles' and Nicene Creeds as witnessing to the mighty acts of God recorded in Scripture,' but they are not to be used 'coercively' as the norm of doctrine. The Bible is vaguely described as the 'unique authority,' which 'witnesses to God's revelation,' rather than God's written word" (*Time,* March 2, 1970, p. 48).

No doubt the existence and work of the C.O.C.U. has precipitated the need for replacement of the N.C.C. It should be kept in mind that the present N.C.C. and C.O.C.U. are not in any conflict. Their ecumenical goals are identical. In fact, their leadership in some cases overlaps.

Increasing theological deterioration and shift from religious matters to political issues in the W.C.C. also indicates the possibility of changes within that Council.

Documentation for August, 1968 carried an article by W. S. McBirnie who attended the W.C.C. Uppsala, Sweden meeting as an observer and newsman. His words deserve serious pondering: "In my opinion the apostasy of leaders and most of the participants in the secondary level of leadership of the World Council of Churches is complete. The group (delegates) cheered the picture of Mao Tse-tung; affirmed that there was no need to evangelize pagan lands (specifically India); affirmed that violence was justified in a revolution when a nation resisted social change; called for dialogue with communists; featured hard-line communist personalities on their program; and condemned 'American aggression in Vietnam,' despite the fact that Americans in Vietnam protect the millions of Christians in South Vietnam against communist butchering. *Time* magazine well said the World Council of Churches in Uppsala was more like a meeting of the New Left than one of clergymen."

The words of Robert Morris, former chief counsel for the Senate Subcommittee on Internal Security of the Senate Judiciary

Committee, are equally as poignant: " . . . it is a shock to me, at least, that the World Council of Churches, meeting in Uppsala, Sweden this week, came forth not only with prime emphasis on very non-spiritual matters but on political declarations that neatly dovetailed with the present importunities of the Communist propaganda mill" (*Wanderer,* August 1, 1968).

Reporting in the *Philadelphia Sunday Bulletin* of June 30. 1968, George W. Cornell referred to the words of Rev. Stephen C. Rose, a Chicago Presbyterian, who said: "Either we invest the council with power and place in the church, or else we admit the failure of the conciliar approach." Cornell then added these prophetic words, "Some church leaders think the coming assembly may be the last for the council, and that rapid ecumenical developments will replace it with a wider forum of churches, embracing Roman Catholicism and smaller evangelical bodies not now members."

A study of ecumenical developments in the Roman Catholic Church in connection with Vatican Council II and between 1961 and 1968 reveal a great deal of progress toward the unification of the W.C.C. and the Roman Catholic Church. Two official reports of the Joint Working Group of the W.C.C. and the Roman Catholic Church were approved by the Uppsala Assembly.

Eugene Carson Blake, who became the second General Secretary of the W.C.C. in 1966, succinctly summarized the present relation of the Roman Catholic Church with the W.C.C. when he said: "The story revealed in these two reports, now approved by the highest authority of both the Roman Catholic Church and the World Council of Churches, is one of almost unbelievable progress and development in a very short time. Consultation and co-operation has rapidly developed in all the major areas of work of the World Council; mission, service, international affairs, youth activity, faith and order, and development activity. The ecumenical story revealed in these two reports is not finished; it has hardly begun. . . . The reports assume that there is only one ecumenical movement and that it is the common task of all Churches and Councils to co-operate in that one movement. This is a revolution which we have witnessed in our time."[21]

---

[21] *The Ecumenical Advance,* p. 441.

The question of actual membership of Rome in the W.C.C. is under serious consideration. Each group wants the other within its confines. To be sure its own attitude is clearly understood, the report of Reference Committee 1 approved by the Uppsala Assembly of the W.C.C. stated: "The Assembly encourages the Joint Working Group to continue to give attention to the question of the membership of the Roman Catholic Church in the World Council of Churches. Membership depends upon the initiative of individual churches willing to accept the basis. The World Council reaffirms its eagerness to extend its membership to include all those Christian Churches at present outside its fellowship."[22]

The Central Committee of the W.C.C. was instructed at the Uppsala Assembly to restructure the W.C.C. in the light of functions which the ecumenical movement now requires. The report asking for this restructuring lists as one of the major considerations to be given attention: "The ramifying partnership with the Roman Catholic Church since Vatican Council II and with other non-member Churches."[23]

Father Roberto Tucci, who addressed the Uppsala Assembly, made it clear that "Roman Catholic ecclesiology did not make membership (in the W.C.C.) impossible." The Assembly itself spoke forthrightly on the subject: "From the side of the World Council of Churches there was in principle, no obstacle to the membership of the Roman Catholic Church in the Council."[24]

We do not know what the next landmark toward church union will be. But one thing is sure—whatever form it takes, it will no doubt be built upon the foundation already laid and will therefore embrace the same unorthodox theology which existing attempts at church union have embraced. The new structure will be one more, perhaps the final, great stride toward the super-church.

C. Stanley Lowell, spokesman for a national organization known as Americans United for Separation of Church and State and author of *The Ecumenical Mirage* gave a report in 1969 to

22*Ibid.*, p. 442.
23*Ibid.*, p. 444.
24*Ibid.*, p. 352.

a conference held in New York City. In the report he said: "It is the obsessive concern with structure that causes apprehension. Church leaders today are not asking what beliefs they have in common as Christians, or what it is they should do together as Christians. They are asking only how they can put together a united, ecclesiastical power structure. This is what the Consultation on Church Union (C.O.C.U.) is diligently seeking and this is the aim of most ecumenical dialogue."

In his closing remarks Lowell presented his view, which this writer shares, of the kind of church which the modern ecumenical movement is building: "Let me share with you what I now see. I see a church rising in our land more powerful than men have known or dreamed. I see a church powerful beyond calculation. I see a church alienated from the people but able to work its will with the state. I see a church so blind with lust for riches and power that it becomes oppressive and subverts the very freedom which is its heart's blood. I see, too, the desperate need for little churchmen and little churches and unchurched, all who will, to stand up to this thing; for those who will rise up to beat it down—to the end that the church may be preserved and that religion of the spirit shall not perish from among us."25

25Cited by Will Oursler, *Protestant Power and the Coming Revolution* (Garden City, New York: Doubleday and Company, Incorporated, 1971), pp. 97, 98.

IV

CONFUSION

There is something drastically wrong with the church when the secular world praises it and applauds it for its "progress." The Christian and the nonchristian have philosophies of life which are diametrically opposed to each other. Scripture reveals the opposition between the two very clearly. The church and the secular world are hostilely at odds with each other. The very nature, purpose, and program of each assures us that this will be the case. This does not mean that those who call themselves Christians and are involved in local churches should seek to make themselves misfits and as miserable as possible. Being disliked by people is no sure sign of being a Christian. It does mean though that because Satan is the god of this age and the prince of this world, because the born-again Christian is a member of the family of God, and because the true church is the church of God; the conflict and animosity of the world against the Christian and the church is inevitable.

Honesty! That is what concerned people with religious interests are asking for and, it would seem, have a right to expect.

The trouble with the ecumenists and promoters of church union or, to put it another way, the theological liberal establishment, is that many of them are not only masters of deceit but are also masters of distortion and confusion. Whatever the reasons may be, one thing is sure, there is evident, wide-scale confusion on the part of church unionists. They are confused and confusing as is evidenced by their practice, program and propaganda. As a natural consequence, their constituents are also confused on some very basic matters. That is the thesis of this chapter. Our purpose will be to spell out various evidences of confusion and in this way to substantiate our thesis.

Basic Facts

Perhaps it would be well to begin with some elemental facts by asking several pertinent questions. When did division begin? Is division really a scandal, the greatest sin which could ever be committed? Does church union really produce health and growth? Who made the first attempts at union?

In answer to the first question it may be said emphatically that division in the church did not begin with the reformers. Ecumenists say that it did. But that is historically false. We are told today by many that the work of the reformers was a great mistake. The Roman Church has always maintained that position, of course; but so does the ecumenical movement. Since Vatican II, Rome has recognized Protestants as separated brethren. Her invitation to Protestantism is to come home—home to Rome, that is. The greatest mistake of the reformers was not that they separated from Rome but that they did not separate completely from the theology and tradition of Rome. It was the persecuted Anabaptists who really maintained strict separation from the Roman Catholic Church. They (Anabaptists) were the first major group to differ with Augustine and Cyprian, early church fathers, over their idea of one visible church outside of which there was no salvation. There simply never has been one visible church as Rome and the Protestant ecumenists claim. Division and separation has marked the visible church from its very beginning. Worthy of note, too, is the fact that the first

great ecumenical councils of the visible church were initiated.
sponsored, and ruled over by the political rulers of the day, not
by the church. They came as the result of Constantine's heretical
notion to Christianize paganism. History reveals that many of
the church fathers complained of division in their day. Usually
division has been not so much because of men but because of
truth.

A quick reply to the question whether division is a scandal
would be, Yes, it is. Upon closer examination, however, that
answer may appear to be too broad and superficial. The assumption, which forms the bedrock foundation for church union and
the one upon which ecumenists operate, is that the bringing
together of all churches into one is the best thing that could
ever happen to the churches. This they insist is the highest good.
It is the will of God. All who get in the way of church unionists
by opposing them are said to be guilty of the "sin of separation."
Without seeking to prove their assumption ecumenists proceed
at breakneck speed to reach their goal. Contrary to the unfounded assumption of those seeking to build a monolithic church, the
Christian faith has spread because of proliferation, not unity.
In fact, the contemporary emphasis upon unity and union has
been responsible for a decline in Christian work and even a loss
in church memberships. Far better to divide, to separate, than to
leave the church in its stagnant sin. Unity and church union are
not supreme virtues. Unifying movements tend to deaden and
stifle the church. They lull people to sleep. Healthy and Biblical
proliferation is an evidence of life and health. Unity at the cost
of truth is not worth having. Certainly some division is unneces-
sary and sinful. But that does not mean it is alway so. "The art
of being like everybody else may be comforting but it is not
stimulating or creative. History teaches that reforms come about
only under challenge and only when the challengers are firm to
the point of proliferation away from the group to be reformed.
That is why division has been good for the church. A church
incapable of proliferation is dead."26

    26C. Stanley Lowell, *The Ecumenical Mirage* (Grand Rapids: Baker Book
House, 1967), p. 83.

A kindred question to the one discussed above is, Have church union movements produced health and growth? And again, with history on our side, we must say, No, they have not. An entirely different picture is painted by those striving for a superchurch. They seek to present a portrait which gives the impression of phenomenal growth and vigor. The facts prove otherwise. To this date the results of mergers have been exactly the opposite of what the ecumenists have promised and their naive devotees have expected. Instead of growth and reproduction of the Christian enterprise there have come a diminishing interest and loss of vigor and vitality because of the bureaucratic control and spiritual dearth of the liberal establishment. With the rise of the ecumenical movement has come the demise of individual distinctives and also the shift in emphasis from missions to mission. It can be no other way! The very basic philosophy of church unionists demands such losses. All faiths are equal, all men are Christian brothers, according to the ecumenists. Therefore, it is not the Christian's nor the church's duty to convert anyone to a particular commitment or faith. Based upon a denial of the exceeding sinfulness of every man and therefore his total lostness and inability to gain favor with God, the church unionists see the role of the church which they are seeking to build as one of education, not one of salvation. Without a completely authoritative message and without a Christ Who is God, the liberal establishment which heads the ecumenical movement has no certain message to give. Contrary of course to the ecumenists, those who reject the ecumenical assumptions and program believe they have a unique message—the gospel, based upon a unique Book—the Bible, about a unique Person—Jesus Christ. They believe that all men are totally and completely lost forever apart from personal faith in Him as Savior. Only one way to Heaven exists, not many. Apart from Jesus Christ there is absolutely no salvation for anyone. The reason for the loss of interest in Biblical missions and evangelism within the ecumenical movement is the loss of a Biblical theology.

Another basic question which deserves answering is: Who made the first attempts toward church union? The proponents of the current ecumenical movement would have the public believe that they did. This is simply not true and only serves to confuse the masses. As we noted in Chapter III, the liberal establishment did not make the first attempts toward bringing Christians together. They were the first ones to cause division and schism within the World Evangelical Alliance which was the first major attempt to unite all evangelical Bible-believing Christians together for a common cause. It was the liberals who could no longer accept the orthodoxy of the Alliance and who separated from the evangelicals to found their own organizations to promote church union among those who rejected the authority of Holy Scripture.

Terminology

Ecumenists have invested traditional and familiar words with new meanings. Without telling the public what they mean by their orthodox-sounding terminology they often succeed in pawning off a bill of goods to Christians and nonchristians. A study of the doctrinal views of those who are promoting church union reveals blatant contradictions between what they believe and the words they use to promote their unbelief. Before accepting at face value what promoters of church union say, the real meaning intended by the vocabulary must be determined. The importance of truth is crucial. Without it words are meaningless. A satanic snare is to get men to invest words with new meanings so that when the old words are uttered they really spell nonsense. Because of the semantic dilusion created by ecumenists, one must raise certain basic questions in his mind whenever church-union enthusiasts use the familiar orthodox language. What kind of God are you presenting when you speak? What do you mean by Scripture? Do you mean by the divinity of Christ, the deity of Christ? You say man must be viewed as a guilty sinner. Does that mean he is really guilty before God or simply that he possesses guilt feelings?

The word *Christian* is used much and very freely in the vocabulary of ecumenists. They do not mean by this term to refer to sinners saved by God's marvelous grace. The Biblical and evangelical meaning of being a disciple of Christ, one who has turned from his sin and from himself to Christ is not intended by the word Christian as used by church unionists. Rather, they use the term to speak of all who embrace some kind of belief in a divine being, power, or influence. They use it to refer to the regenerate born-again believers and also to those who make no such claims and in fact repudiate the very idea.

Another word which comes in for much usage is the word *church*. Along with that is also the word *churches*. There is a crass failure to distinguish between the church and the churches. In fact, this is one of the most basic failures of ecumenists. They pretend and proclaim that the visible church they are building is identical with the one true invisible Church of Scripture. The Bible does speak of the Church which is Christ's Body and also of local assemblies to whom many of the New Testament books were addressed. Church unionists fail to distinguish between these two. They speak as though all who claim the name Christian for themselves are such and are therefore a part of the Church.

Robert G. Torbet, ecumenist and Executive Director of the Division of Cooperative Christianity of the American Baptist Convention and an observer-consultant for the American Baptist Convention to the C.O.C.U., voiced this confusion among ecumenists when he said: "This distinction made by the Free Churches between the church invisible and universal and a church visible and local cannot be supported by the New Testament."27

Even though the ecumenical liberal establishment has rejected the authority of the Bible and all the crucial doctrines of the orthodox Christian faith, it still views itself as the Church, the Body of Christ. There is complete failure to recognize that not every organization which carries the label *church* is necessarily a part of the Body of Christ. Scripture teaches that the local church is to be a miniature of the universal Church of which all who are born-again are members. It also teaches that no one can be a part of the Body of Christ who has not been born-again through faith in Jesus Christ. Multitudes of Chris-

---

27Robert G. Torbet, *Ecumenism . . . Free Church Dilemma* (Valley Forge, Pennsylvania: The Judson Press, 1968), p. 110.

tians are familiar with such language. When ecumenists retain the language but change the meaning, nothing but planned confusion results.

Use of Scripture

Strange indeed that the ecumenists, who reject the authority of Scripture and call evangelicals who believe it obscurantists and extreme literalists, are the very ones who repeatedly seek to bolster their attempts by an appeal to a few "proof texts" of Scripture. There are two favorite and prominent passages in the vocabulary of those pushing for church union. One cannot help but believe they are used deceptively—only to satisfy evangelicals by pretending to be doing the solemn will of God upon scriptural authority.

Torn from its setting completely a small phrase from John 17:21 is used most frequently: "That they all may be one." As used by the ecumenists and without considering the context in which the phrase is found, it sounds very impressive. Two glaring contradictions reveal the absurd fallacy of such a usage of the passage. The first is that the liberal establishment, which heads the ecumenical drive, does not accept the Bible as the very Word of God. How then is it possible to suddenly draw upon a portion of that Word to give divine sanction to their claims and to use a text of Scripture as the all-embracing goal, purpose, and slogan of their movement? The second contradiction is that only by a process of tortured exegesis can John 17:20 through 23 be made to teach what the ecumenical leaders imply it teaches.

The passage says nothing about organizational union of all religious groups and denominations into one great monolithic structure. God the Son Who is engaged in prayer to God the Father in this passage has just completed instructing His disciples concerning their responsibilities and privileges in light of His imminent death. He has spoken to them concerning the need for humility (John 13), the promise and comfort of the coming Holy Spirit (John 14), fruitbearing and its requirements (John 15), and the new work of the Holy Spirit (John 16). In His prayer recorded in John 17 He prays these truths home to the Father. First, He prays for Himself (17:1-8). Second, He prays for the disciples, Judas being absent (17:9-19). Third, He prays for all those who will believe on Him because of the faithfulness of His disciples (17:20-26). The *flock* to be united is spoken of as "these," the ones given to Him by the Father. The *foundation* of the unity for which He prays is given in verse 11: "Holy Father, keep through thine own name those whom thou has given me. . . . " Nowhere in this prayer does our Lord exhort men to produce unity. His simple request is that the Father would keep the unity which was already in existence and which the Son had kept while He was in the world. Here the Savior spoke with certainty as though the baptizing-identifying work of the Holy Spirit were already a reality though that did not take place until the Day of Pentecost (Acts 2). Christ also presents in this high-priestly prayer the *formula* for the unity which He sustained and now the Father is beseeched to sustain. He clearly identifies the nature of the unity. It is to be "as we are," "as thou Father art in me" (17:11, 21). This relates to the unity within the Godhead. Who would deny that the Father and the Son were and are One in doctrine (i.e. John 7:16; 8:26, 28; 12:49), devotion (John 6:38, 40; 17:4), and in demonstration of love (John 17:23)? Surely this prayer of Christ is not to be answered by Bible-rejecting, Christ-rejecting ecumenists who are seeking to build a superchurch. The prayer has already been answered by the Father to Whom it was addressed. Through the death of Christ, the One Who prayed, the middle wall of partition was broken down (Eph. 2:15-18). All who have accepted Him as their Sin-bearer are "one in Christ" (Gal. 3:28). All such have been "baptized into one body" (1 Cor. 12:13). They therefore all have "One Lord, one faith, one baptism, One God and Father of all. . . " (Eph. 4:4-6).

Undeniably, it is necessary for God's children to manifest this oneness in Christ in a visible way if the world of lost men is to know that God sent His Son and that He loves them (John 17:23). Believers have failed miserably at this task. This is not to say, however, that the manifestation of this oneness is to be seen by believer and nonbeliever joining hands in spiritual endeavors or by the building of a great superchurch with a highly organized unbelieving bureaucracy in control.

The second passage of Scripture used most frequently by ecumenists to buttress their efforts is Ephesians 4:1 through 16. Various phrases such as "the unity of the Spirit," "one body," "the whole body" appear often in the language of ecumenists. Again, they are torn from the context in which they are found. Professional ecumenists would have us believe the Apostle Paul was saying that church union is the all-important thing, taking precedence even over doctrine. Their philosophy is that it really does not matter what you believe so long as you express love for one another. Joining hands with those with whom you have serious doctrinal differences and disagreements will eventually produce the unity of the faith. These inspired words from the Apostle Paul teach no such thing. The fact is, they teach exactly the opposite—doctrine comes before fellowship. This is evident by noting carefully the opening words of verse 1: "I therefore." Immediately, this takes us back to what was said previously. The emphasis upon unity presented in chapter 4 is a natural consequence of what has been said before and is based squarely upon it. Chapters 1 through 3 of Ephesians are filled with great doctrinal themes. The sovereign purposes and work of God in the salvation of sinners are discussed in chapter 1. The helplessness of man to save himself is clearly evident there (1:4-6). So is the substitutionary work of Christ made known (1:7), as is man's need to trust Him (1:12, 13). Chapter 2 is even more specific about the inability of man to do anything to merit favor with God (2:1, 5, 8-10). Throughout the first three chapters the uniqueness of Christ as God's Son and man's only Savior is stressed repeatedly. Some of those very doctrines which the ecumenists reject most are dealt with here by Paul. Exhortation is given then to those who had experienced the work of salvation to "keep the unity of the Spirit in the bond of peace" (4:3). Not some fabricated organizational unity, but the unity of the Spirit is to be kept. Again, as in Christ's prayer, Paul relates this unity to that unity which characterizes the Trinity (4:4-6). The Ephesians are not told to create unity but to "keep" the unity which already exists. They were to live in keeping with their family relationship. Even though members of the family of God possess different gifts, they are not to major on minors but to find their strength and help from each other by remembering that they all have the things that matter most in common. The passage stresses the appeal to "keep" the unity of the spirit (4:1-3), the nature of the unity (4:4-6), variety in unity (4:7-12), and the future full realization of that unity (4:13-16).

Unity is one thing! Union is another! These terms are mutilated and misused by ecumenists. By virtue of the gracious work of God through Christ every believing sinner is a member of the family of God. Those same believing sinners are also vitally related not only to all the members of the family but also to every member of the Godhead. What greater unity could there be than that? Such a unity cannot be earned, it is not deserved; but it is a real spiritual unity nonetheless. Organizational union sought after by ecumenists has not a trifle of support in Scripture. The prayer of Christ recorded in John 17 was answered by the sovereign work of the Spirit. Children of God are now called upon to "keep" this spiritual unity because of the great doctrinal oneness which brought them and keeps them in the family of God. This is far removed from what the current cry for church union is proposing.

Doctrinal Beliefs

Without any fixed meaning attached to the scanty doctrinal statements, none of the existing arms of the church union movement can be expected to have within their fold any theological norm. They do not want it and they surely do not have it. A perusal of the doctrinal beliefs of the constituents of the W.C.C., N.C.C., and C.O.C.U. makes this very clear. One of the major results of such a hodgepodge of theological views on basic tenets of Christianity is confusion. The place where the confusion is the worst is on the lay level of the member denominations. Such a doctrinal mixture accounts for the varied responses toward the ecumenical movement on the part of church members.

Creedless organizations can produce only confusion. That is, without any standard means of testing for membership only a wide range of doctrinal viewpoints ranging from orthodoxy to heterodoxy can be expected. Often the rank unbelief of the liberal church-union establishment is covered with a plethora of orthodox-sounding words. Some, like the late Bishop Pike, one of the founding fathers of C.O.C.U. and an active ecumenist, do not try to hide their unbelief. Said he, "The kind of God, I first believed in, who would limit salvation to a select group of people who happened to have heard the news and heard it well, is an impossible God. As to this God, I am now an atheist."

Such views on basic issues affect every facet of church life. Considering the amalgamation of doctrinal views represented in the N.C.C. it is little wonder that a new concept of evangelism has emerged. At a meeting in Atlanta, in May, 1965, "The National Council of Churches Commission on Evangelism spent their sessions discussing race relations and experimental ministries that seek to serve men rather than convert them" (*Time*, May 14, 1965). The doubt and denial of the cardinal doctrines of the faith by professed churchmen has sent such unbelief and unconcern to the pew. Why not? As the pastor goes, so go the people!

Communism Versus Christianity

Mention has already been made of the influence and involvement of communism in the organizations striving for church union. Reference to this fact again is to highlight another means of confusion perpetuated by the ecumenical movement. Concerned evangelicals have for years insisted that the communists have infiltrated the church, especially through the N.C.C. and W.C.C., and that these organizations are soft toward communism. They have substantiated their claims with reliable documentation including the reports of the F.B.I. and the House Committee on Un-American Activities and many other means. These have been denied by church-union activists. But the facts remain as stark evidences to the contrary.

The Communist Party has made common cause with the liberal establishment on several fronts. A classic example is the eighteenth National Convention of the Communist Party, U.S.A. in New York City. There party leaders and agents active both in leftist and liberal organizations were ordered to work for the racio-religious identification of everyone in the nation. This represents a change in policy in keeping with the Party's ten-year plan for taking the U.S.A. into the Soviet World Government by July 4, 1976. The Party has assigned the task to its agents of encouraging and giving impetus to an amalgamation of religious bodies which Russia has planned will result in a universal "Church of World Brotherhood" (*The American Mercury*, Winter, 1966). The communists want up-to-date data to chart such a church merger. This also may account for the apparent shift in communism from a hostile to a tolerant position toward religion recently. At the eighteenth National Convention of the Communist Party, U.S.A. "Godless Religion" was a part of what they called "Operation 76." The communist plan for a Soviet-dominated World State by July 4, 1776 fits well into their hopes for a superchurch by the mid 1970's. The Soviet plan fits in well with the N.C.C. and W.C.C. interfaith approach. The social gospel which these two organizations and the sister C.O.C.U. movement promote includes closer church-state relations. This is evident in their promotion of racial and religious integration, huge federal aid programs to private institutions, urban renewal programs, and countless resolutions which have little or nothing to do with religious matters and instead are designed to pressure the federal government into closer relationship to the church. Also, the ecumenical message includes a totally new concept of the worship of God. Social involvement and even the new morality of situation ethics are considered forms of worship.

Such activities which fit the communist take-over plan beautifully continue to isolate those who are not in favor of ecumenism and who oppose it. This also seems to be part of the plan. It is predicted that this will increase and continue until the federal government will find it necessary to step in. By virtue of past activities and sheer force of power from the numerical representation, agencies such as the N.C.C. and the W.C.C. will force the federal government to determine the eligibility of tax exemption, etc., of such men and movements who do not meet the liberal establishment's requirements on the basis of their creed. "A 'church' or 'religious body' or 'religious practitioner' will be defined in terms of the N.C.C.'s 'creed' of a secular God, the social gospel and the new morality. Bodies and individuals deviating from this 'creed' whether N.C.C. affiliated or not, are to be excluded from the exemptions granted their income and property in previous years, and the contributors to such nonconformists will be restricted and taxed (or denied deductions) on the monies and property which they give or bequeath to the same" (*The American Mercury*, Winter, 1966).

What does all of this mean to the layman? It means that if and when these plans are fully realized, hard times await the evangelical believer. It also means that there is evidence to indicate that the communists' "Operation 76" plan parallels and supplements the plan and strategy of the thrust for a superchurch. The softness of the ecumenical movement toward communism serves to confuse Christianity and communism. The two are made to appear almost synonymous. The goal of atheistic communism has been and continues to be advanced by those seeking to unite all religious faiths. All evidence points to the fact that communist conspiracy is using the ecumenical movement to advance its cause. Paralleling this there is also substantial evidence that many responsible leaders of the ecumenical movement are communist sympathizers. This is not something just recently discovered either. The controversy in 1960 over the *U.S. Air Force Reserve Training Manual* brought much of this to light. The manual was protested by church groups and Congress investigated. The church groups did not like the warning sounded by the manual that communists and their sympathizers had infiltrated into churches. During the hearings, Richard Arens, then staff director of the House Committee on Un-American Activities, testified. His testimony is startling: "Thus far of the leadership of the National Council of Churches of Christ in America, we have found over 100 persons in leadership capacity with either Communist-front records or records of service to Communist causes. The aggregate affiliations of the leadership, instead of being in the hundreds as first indicated, is now, according to the latest count, into the thousands, and we have yet to complete our check, which would certainly suggest, on the basis of authoritative sources of this committee, that the statement that there is infiltration of fellow travelers in churches and educational institutions is a complete understatement."[28] Significantly enough, the recent statement of the U.S. Communist Party Chief, Gus Hall, substantiates this evidence when he said that the communist goals for America are "almost identical" to those of the liberal church.

The Church's Role

Just what is the church commissioned to do? What is its major task? Is it spiritual or is it political? What was the relation of the church of New Testament times to the political world in which it found itself? Students of the Bible know that it teaches a clear separation between church and state. The Christian is to obey them that rule over him. He is to be subject to the higher powers because they are ordained of God. Disobedience to civil authority is only sanctioned in Scripture when that authority forces disobedience to God. We are to obey God rather than man.

The church is a spiritual institution ordained of God to propagate the gospel to the lost and to provide spiritually for the children of God. Contrary to this clearly delineated Biblical purpose, the liberal ecumenical movement, as represented in the liberal church councils, has gone political. Alteration of the social order through political action rates high on its priority list.

Dr. Espy, General Secretary of the N.C.C., expressed his view of the role of the church or the church's task this way: "Not only is this God's creation, but God speaks through what we call the secular manifestations of his creation. He manifests himself in secular history and in contemporary secular events, and he manifests himself in this way to the life of the church. And the church needs to try to hear God's voice through the world around it just as much probably as through the activity that takes place within the cloistered walls of the religious institution itself." He said the church must come "to be engaged with the life of humanity and not simply the life of the church per se as we've been accustomed to understand it."[29]

28Issues Presented by the Air Reserve Training Manual, Hearings, HCUA, February 25, 1960.

29Oursler, *op. cit.*, pp. 11, 12.

It will not be necessary to deal here with the multitude of pronouncements issued by the N.C.C. and the W.C.C. relative to political action. Recent policy statements of these two organizations will be sufficient to illustrate the unbiblical role which church unionists are assigning to the church. Evidence of widespread concern and confusion on the part of many over what is taking place in the N.C.C. and W.C.C. became public by a full-page advertisement in the *New York Times* for November 18, 1968. Other daily newspapers carried the same ad later. Sponsored by the Clergymen's Committee on China, the ad, signed by thousands of clergymen, stated the cause for concern and confusion on the part of millions of Americans: "1. The political and economic drift to the left by the National and World Council of Churches; 2. The recent statements of U.S. Communist Party Chief, Gus Hall, that Red goals for America are 'almost identical' to those espoused by the *Liberal Church*; 3. Their realization that the expressed convictions of the National and World Councils of Churches so frequently, over such a long period of time, with communist ideology; 4. The open effort being made to soften up church people to accept Communism as merely another liberal movement."

The ad went on to list the recommendations of the General Board of the National Council of Churches made at its meeting on February 21, 1968: "1. Stop the bombing of North Vietnam as a prelude to seeking a negotiated peace. 2. Avoid provocative military actions against Mainland China in the knowledge that it has legitimate interests in Asia. 3. Press for the admission of Mainland China into the United Nations. 4. Create conditions for cooperation between the United States and the Communist countries of Eastern Europe, the Soviet Union and Cuba. 5. Recognize the Government of Cuba and acknowledge the existence of the East German Democratic Republic. 6. Remove restrictions on imports from Communist countries and on cultural exchanges between the United States and the Soviet Union."

In the same advertisement the recommendations and pronouncements of the July, 1968 Uppsala meeting of the W.C.C. were also listed: "1. *Granting recognition to Red China*, stating that her entrance into the international community (U.N.) is a 'matter of great significance to the future of mankind.' 2. *Adoption* of the idea of 'One World Government,' by suggesting that 'Christians should urge their governments to accept the rulings of the International Court of Justice without reservation.' 3. *Endorsement* of the principles of world socialism by advocating the Marxist philosophy of 'from each according to his ability, to each according to his need.' The idea of a tax of 1% of G.N.P. [Gross National Product] for industrialized countries was presented as a means of accomplishing this. 4. '*The lifting of the economic blockade of Cuba,* as an example of what could be done to develop a political climate which can adopt development policies transcending purely ideological and political interests.' 5. '*The immediate and unconditional' cessation of all U.S. bombing of North Vietnam,* and the use of all weapons of mass destruction. 6. Endorsement of 'the principle of civil disobedience of draft laws by conscientious objectors and giving sanction to non-participation in particular wars for reason of conscience.' "

Such policy statements are exemplary of the actions of church unionists for many years. They also serve to demonstrate the utter confusion produced by ecumenists in the activities they have involved the churches they represent.

Violence and Moral Decay

There is something terribly wrong when a religious spokesman for hundreds of thousands of churchgoers tells militant student agitators to go further in their menacing activities. Yet that is what the president of the National Council of Churches did at a symposium on International Student Militancy. He said, "I think student activists can and should go further than they have" (Religious News Service, November 22, 1968). Little wonder then that the leadership of denominations affiliated with the N.C.C. should adopt similar views. This many of them have done.

In June 1968 a motion was approved overwhelmingly by the N.C.C. General Assembly which put the Council behind what it prefers to call non-violent disobedience. The resolution said, "We recognize that when justice cannot be secured either through action within the existing structures or through civil disobedience an increasing number of Christians may feel called to seek justice through resistance or revolution."[30]

As a result of such pronouncements confusion, distrust, and strife have settled upon the lay public. Many do not understand. Others refuse to believe what they hear. Some naively accept what their leaders say thinking the clergy should know more about such matters than they do. They do not think it worth arguing about. Still others become terribly disturbed and friction results between people in the pew and between those in the pew and the pulpit and denominational headquarters. A recent example of this is in the United Methodist Church. The denomination adopted a very controversial stand on civil disobedience. Later, delegates to the Central Texas Methodist Conference adopted a resolution asking their national denomination to amend its stand favoring civil disobedience which they contended encouraged and sanctioned bloodshed and arson.[31] Three days after the assassination of Senator Robert F. Kennedy, the Associated Press reported from New York that the general board of the National Council of Churches had adopted a policy statement approving peaceable civil disobedience. "The board in a statement yesterday on 'religious obedience and civil disobedience' said that civil disobedience means deliberate peaceable violation of a law deemed unjust in relation to conscience or a higher law." Other news media also made reference to the N.C.C.'s action and position on civil disobedience in bold statements. Religious News Service reported that civil disobedience as defined by such men as Gandhi and Martin Luther King, Jr., was recognized by the N.C.C. as "a valid instrument for those who seek justice."[32] Not infrequently the N.C.C. has taken the side of agitators against the police departments. *U. S. News and World Report* states in quoting a commission of the N.C.C. that student violence is to be condoned because "God is some way present in these movements."

The World Council of Churches consultation on racism meeting in London, May, 1969 recommended that "The world's

---

[30]*Ibid.*, p. 9.
[31]*Dallas Times Herald,* May 28, 1969.
[32]*Ibid.*, June 7, 1968.

churches should support violence if it is the last way to over-throw political and economic tyranny."[33] According to the United Press International report of May 24, the W.C.C. consultation received a delegation representing the Student Nonviolent Co-ordinating Committee. This delegation voiced demands for $144 million from white churches to defend arrested Black Power militants and to encourage revolutionary movements such as the Viet Cong. Eugene Carson Blake, General Secretary of the Council and father of C.O.C.U., reportedly told them the W.C.C. consultation was not as far from some of their demands as they might think. The demands were to be referred to the Central Committee of the W.C.C. for possible action.

Bewilderment and fear have come upon many because of the demands of James Foreman for $500 million in reparations from the white religious community. This initial request has been upped considerably because of apparent success. The "Black Manifesto" he delivered was presented to the N.C.C. and its message was accepted by it. The N.C.C. asked its constituents to give it "serious" attention. "Ironically, this blunt demand on the churches originated from a well-intentioned effort by a liberal interfaith group to draw out black ideas for the economic better-ment of urban ghettos. The Interreligious Foundation for Com-munity Organization (IFCO), which includes twenty-three Prot-estant, Catholic, Jewish, Negro, and Mexican-American groups, organized the National Black Economic Development Confer-ence to bring black leaders together for discussions and action on the economic aspects of Black Power. . . . By week's end the General Board of the National Council of Churches had record-ed its 'deep appreciation' to Foreman and avowed that it 'shares the aspirations of the black people of this country' " (*Time*, May 16, 1969). Member churches of the N.C.C. such as the United Methodist and others have already made sizeable contributions to meet the demands of the Black Manifesto. Apparently, trying to protect itself from too much criticism from the right the N.C.C. has recognized that it does not agree with the "ideology" of Foreman's Black Manifesto. Contrary to that, however, the

---

[33]*Ibid.*, May 25, 1969.

N.C.C. has made arrangements to contribute to his demands. Financial and moral support by the Council is difficult to explain if it is not in sympathy with Foreman and his Black Manifesto. In fact, any question regarding the N.C.C.'s view of the Black Manifesto should be removed by its action in September, 1969. The General Board of the N.C.C. met at that time in Indianapolis, Indiana and refused to denounce the organization issuing the Manifesto. At the same meeting the N.C.C. urged its constituents to raise the amount Foreman requested and give it to the Interreligious Foundation for Community Organization (IFCO) and to the National Committee of Black Churchmen (NCBC). Both of these groups are related to Foreman and his Manifesto.

What is even more alarming than the N.C.C.'s reaction to the Black Manifesto is the view of many evangelicals. The U.S. Congress on Evangelism held in Minneapolis in September, 1969 had those on its platform who also endorsed the Manifesto. It is difficult to understand how those who are evangelicals and who are aligned with evangelical organizations could support that which clearly calls for revolution and has as its aim the bringing down of this country to establish "a society where the total means of production are taken from the rich and placed into the hands of the state for the welfare of all the people." Such anti-scriptural views and action sponsored by church organizations dedicated to the building of a superchurch evidences the confusion of purpose and program on the part of all involved.

Sanction of civil disobedience is often coupled with sanction of immorality by church union enthusiasts. Since objective, absolute truth has been spurned, this is not a surprising development. The standards of right and wrong clearly outlined in Scripture have been replaced with a philosophy which says, "If you love each other, anything goes." The N.C.C. published a booklet in 1961 for the United Christian Youth Movement. The booklet is entitled, *Called to Responsible Freedom, The Meaning of Sex in the Christian Life.* In it the youth are told " . . . for the Christian there are no laws, no rules, no regulations. . . . Life is a series of grays and not pure blacks and whites" (pp. 6, 7). *Campus Encounter* is a magazine published by the United Campus Christian

Fellowship which is the campus movement of the Disciples of Christ, Evangelical United Brethren (now United Methodist), United Church of Christ and the United Presbyterian Church in the U.S.A. The Winter, 1965, edition of this periodical included an article entitled "Love Without Fear." Even some postmasters would not accept such immoral filth as the article contained. The author pictured, with complete approval, a society where there would be no sexual restrictions or inhibitions whatsoever. *The Christian Century* magazine, mouthpiece for the liberal ecumenical establishment, made its view clear regarding sex. The Reverend Gordon Clanton, a Presbyterian clergyman, argued there that sexual intercourse outside of marriage should not be condemned by the church. Said he, it "can be good. It appears that it already is good for some people, and it can be good for others if the church will bring the gospel to bear on post-Pill sexuality" (January 8, 1969). Some even go so far as to call the "new morality" Christian (*United Church Herald,* May, 1969). Perhaps the high point of such moral decay was manifested in the film, "Another Pilgrim," prepared and shown for the W.C.C.'s Uppsala, Sweden meeting. Such debauchery in the name of Christianity, showing a minister removing his clothes, has yet to reach its full impact upon the professing church.

Oursler, who presents a frank and frightening account of the ecumenical movement and the coming revolution in his book, *Protestant Power and the Coming Revolution,* cites an example of the inroads of moral decay. "The role of shock seemingly for its own sake—is a recurrent explosive factor in the new breed of religion. One fragmentary example of the kind of activity that began to become increasingly familiar in the late 1960's is seen in a report from St. Louis, Missouri, where the United Methodists held a 'convocation on worship' attended by more than two thousand persons.

"A minister who addressed this convocation regarding worship methods in his West Coast ecumenical church was quoted as saying:

"'In every service . . . we embrace one another. We kiss one another. We feel one another.'

"'Most of our people believe in the communal life. I have

not married a single couple [at my church] who were not already living together.'

" 'One qualification for our secretaries . . . is that they be sexy and wear mini-skirts. If a woman is sexually desirable, why not tell her so?'

" 'We had one of our girls who had given birth to a child out of wedlock stand before our church and tell the inner joy of having a baby without moral inhibitions.'

" 'People become stimulated in our church happenings. We believe in people doing their thing and doing what they want to. Several have become so stimulated . . . they have disrobed. One young man came to church covered only by a blanket. During the service he walked up front and threw his blanket down and stood there totally naked. I walked over and patted him and said, "Man, what a beautiful body you have." ' "34

One cannot help but ask the question: Why such approval of violence and immorality on the part of church officials? No doubt the answer is many-sided. One thing is sure. The relation between communism and the ecumenical movement accounts for much of this attempt to destroy and demoralize America and the Christian principles upon which it was founded.

34Oursler, *op. cit.*, pp. 16, 17.

V

GOALS

A significant number of people remain unconvinced, or at least uncertain, of the real goal of the ecumenical movement. This is understandable since the organizations associated with the ecumenical movement and the liberal establishment which controls them deny any ulterior motive. Both the W.C.C. and the N.C.C. have disavowed any desire to build a superchurch. All their efforts have failed to allay the fears of many. There is too much evidence to the contrary. We have already referred to the drive for a superchurch on the part of the ecumenists. Documentation has been presented to support the proposition. The purpose of this chapter is to solidify earlier inferences of this and to present more undeniable evidence of the goal of ecumenists—creation of one church for one world. This has been the theme and dream of ecumenists. All else including unity of doctrine must take second place. The all-important thing for ecumenists is to have all men under one organizational structure.

Illustrative of the denials of the N.C.C. and W.C.C. to become a superchurch appeared in an article in the liberal *Chris-*

tian Century, February 1, 1961, entitled "No Superchurch but Superfellowship." James Wagner, the author, reiterated the denials and then contradicted what he said by revealing the way in which the future church can be healthy. He said, "The future health of the 'holy catholic church' can be assured only by outgrowing our various traditions, not by a brusque break with them." Interestingly enough, the very next issue of the same ecumenical journal carried an article entitled "The Church and Unity" by Gerald Kennedy. In it he said, "Indeed, the desirability of all churches becoming one has now attained the status of a proposition which no right thinking man should deny."

For years even the secular press has brought attention to the goal of the ecumenical movement. Many articles have appeared in newspapers and periodicals stating the ecumenical goal very clearly. The public is getting the message even though ecumenical agencies insist they are not delivering it. Where did *U.S. News and World Report* ever get the idea for an article like "Superchurch: When Will We Have It?" (July 25, 1966) or *Time,* "Ecumenism, Toward a Superchurch" (March 28, 1969)? If ecumenists do not intend to build a superchurch, why do leaders and those who are involved in ecumenical movements write books defending such a concept? How is the public to relate titles such as "World Christianity," "Toward a United Church," "The Coming Great Church," "Concerns of the World Church," "One Christ, One World, One Church," "Tomorrow's Church: Catholic, Evangelical, Reformed," etc., etc., to the disclaim of the N.C.C. and W.C.C.? If these titles do not mean what they say, then what do they mean? The fact is the denials of the ecumenists are simply not true.

Douglas Horton, no friend of independency, said of the establishment of the N.C.C. in 1950, "The members of the various groups involved were too fully occupied with the subjects at hand to realize that a delicate orientation was taking place within them. They were actually, under the guidance of the Spirit, becoming members of a world church, itself in the process of formation" (*Moody Monthly,* December, 1966).

An opponent of ecumenism and the superchurch idea has touched upon the glaring conflict between the denials of ecumenists of building a superchurch and what is obviously taking place but is often overlooked by laymen. "The modern Super-church already in existence—(1) Claims no official authority over its constituent members although actually exercising that authority in subtle and invisible ways. (2) Has no detailed creed, because the Establishment has completely repudiated the idea that doctrinal unity is essential to centralized ecclesiastical government. (3) Makes no claim to apostolic or Biblical authority since it repudiates both. It claims rather, direct relationship with the Holy Spirit which supercedes both. (4) Levies no financial assessments on local congregations, because its budget is underwritten by its constituent denominations. (5) Needs no members, because its central oligarchy rules through satellite councils and appropriate corporate bodies. (6) Does not baptize, for baptism is not essential to its membership or fellowship. (7) Has no liturgy or eucharist for the same reason. (8) Has no local churches or parishes because it can control all the local churches and parishes of its constituent members in all matters essential to its welfare. (9) Trains no clergy because it supervises and controls all educational processes by which this work is done. (10) Does not bear the name of a church, because it is the channel through which the ultimate Ecumenical church—One Church for One World—will be achieved. When that church comes into full flower there will be no need for the National Council."[35]

Ecumenists would have us believe that times have changed and a kind of superchurch is possible without the well-known essentials. Too, what the ecumenical leaders mean by the superchurch they insist they are not building, and what the Christian lay public understands by the superchurch in the making may be two entirely different things. Granted a multitude of changes will necessarily take place within the existing church structures of the denominations associated with the ecumenical movement before a superchurch is fully developed. In fact, the future superchurch will hardly be identifiable with anything now in existence. Present trends indicate that it will be a monolithic superstructure engulfing a multitude of religious beliefs under a highly

---

[35]James DeForest Murch, *The Protestant Revolt* (Arlington, Virginia: Crestwood Books, 1967) , pp. 47, 48.

organized echelon of leaders with a "pope" at the head. Already
Protestant sponsors of church union have made public their
acceptance of the idea of the present pope or some future one
being the titular head of the envisioned church. The conditioning process has already begun. Preparation of the Protestant lay
public to rethink its traditional view of the unscriptural role of
the pope is presently in process. "Protestants should presuppose
now that the reunited church of the future will be equipped with
a papal office and a college of bishops" (*Journal of Ecumenical
Studies,* Winter, 1968).

The Director of Ecumenical Affairs for the N.C.C. spelled
out quite specifically some of the basic issues relative to the
superchurch of the future. He said, "My thesis can be put quite
simply: that the day has arrived to declare the existence of a
general church membership. This means that, if you become a
Christian other Christians acknowledge that you are fully a
Christian. It is unrealistic, of course, to expect all Christians to
accept such a principle at the start. There will be inevitable
regional and ideological holdouts. But the norm at least, let us
say, among the ten churches which now comprise the Consultation on Church Union and the Roman Catholic Church and the
Lutheran Church in America will be that anyone who belongs
to one belongs to all" (*The Christian Century,* September 11,
(1968). No doubt the Consultation on Church Union will produce the first stage of the superchurch. Ten "guidelines" for the
structure of a proposed united church have already been drawn
up. The General Secretary for C.O.C.U., Paul A. Crow, Jr., has
stated clearly that something "irreversible" has begun in C.O.C.U.
He also stated at a news conference that the issue is not "*if,* but
when church union, will take place, and *who.*"

The Secretary Secretariat for Promoting Christian Unity
from Vatican City, J. G. M. Willebrands, was a guest speaker at
the March, 1969, C.O.C.U. meeting. Among other very favorable
remarks concerning the entrance of the Roman Catholic Church
into C.O.C.U. he said, "It is encouraging to see the C.O.C.U.
desire not merely 'to form a new and larger denomination, but
to embark on a pilgrimage whose Only Ultimate Goal can be the
Unity of the Whole Body." C.O.C.U. is not secretive about the

fact that when the "plan of union" is adopted the churches involved will become one church. The point of no return will then have been reached.

The ambition for a superchurch did not start, of course, with C.O.C.U. The old Federal Council of Churches was not only labeled "socialist" and "pacifist" by U.S. Naval Intelligence, but *Newsweek* referred to it as "a virtual monopoly" which was seeking authority over all its members. The W.C.C. and N.C.C. have advanced and expanded the initial attempts of the F.C.C. Added impetus and perhaps even a shortcut was given to the superchurch goal by the formation of C.O.C.U.

Without question, Samuel McCrea Cavert, former Executive Secretary in the U.S.A. for the W.C.C. and General Secretary of the N.C.C., spelled out the goal of the ecumenical movement. "This would, however, require radical changes in the conception of a denomination's authority. It would call for firm agreements between the denominations which would limit their independence to the extent of assuring to the Christian community as a whole a common membership, a common ministry, common sacraments, and a common organ of co-ordinated action."[36]

The fundamental question for the Bible-believing Christian in response to all such talk is: Does Holy Scripture really teach that there should be one visible organized church on earth? Ecumenists base their whole approach on the unfounded assumption that it does. At least they brainwash the conservative element in their movement to believe their goal is Biblically based. Non-ecumenists insist that there is not a shred of Biblical evidence to support such an assumption. Church unionists attempt to find Biblical sanction for their unbiblical goal by speaking of their "oneness in Christ" in spite of the present "disunity as churches." The fact is, there can be no "oneness in Christ" apart from personal faith in the substitutionary death of the Christ of Scripture and the regenerating work of the Holy Spirit. Since the liberal ecumenical endeavor includes those who deny the authority of Scripture and the deity of Christ along with many other cardinal essentials of the Christian faith, how can there be

---

[36]Samuel McCrea Cavert, *On the Road to Christian Unity* (New York: Harper Brothers, 1961), pp. 159, 160.

"oneness in Christ" within the group? There is no doctrinal oneness nor Biblical oneness in the organizations advocating church
union.

The building of a superchurch is not the only goal of church
unionists. Paralleling that goal and closely associated with it is
the dream of a world government. Edmund A. Opitz, foe of ecumenism and senior staff member of the Foundation for Economic
education, presented their ambition bluntly. He said, "Influential churchmen and theologians, operating through official church
agencies and organizations, have strained to the task of molding
the Protestant churches into a politically potent Great Church
for the Great Society. Their joint efforts have not been for the
attainment of Christian unity for its own sake; it has been unity-
for-the-sake-of-power."[37] No more blatant contradiction of the
historically American and Protestant position of the separation
of church and state and the need for civil obedience can be
found than that produced at the 1966 Conference of Church and
Society sponsored by the W.C.C. The prospectus from that conference said: "In cases where legislation violates an acceptable
constitution and no speedy means of legal relief are available,
the Christian may be called to civil disobedience (sit-down strikes,
passive disobedience or deliberate violation of laws). In cases in
which the constitution itself is inadequate, the Christian is called
to work for its amendment in the interest of firmer guarantees of
human rights. Where such changes are impossible, the Christian
may come to the conclusion that he has no alternative but to
violate the constitution in order to make possible a better one. . .
Laws may be defied in the defense of the constitution, and the
constitution may be defied in defense of human rights."[38]

The radical pronouncements of the conference should fright-
en every true child of God. The results of the conference were
not accidental either. Four years of planning and preparation by
W.C.C. personnel went into it. Not only was there high praise

---

[37]Kenneth W. Ingwalson, compiler, *Your Church—Their Target* (Arlington, Virginia: Better Books Publisher, 1966) , p. 95.
[38]Murch, *op. cit.*, p. 76.

for Communist Russia and China but also attacks were made upon America calling for world revolution. The secular press in this country had headlines descriptive of the violent and revolutionary challenges of the conference. One of the stated purposes of the conference was "to show the churches what their particular task is in shaping a responsible society. . . " and " . . . to help the churches to become responsible partners in making the decisive choices concerning the future developments of society." M. H. Reynolds, Jr., reporter at the conference for the American Council of Christian Churches, called it "The Ecumenical Blueprint For a World Socialist-Communist Revolution." He said the W.C.C. conference program called for "World Government, World Taxation, World Law, a World Court and a World Church while attacking patriotism, nationalism and fidelity to the fundamentals of the Christian faith and doctrine."

A one-church-one-world ring comes from the words of Eugene Carson Blake, the father of C.O.C.U., when he said at the W.C.C.'s Uppsala, Sweden meeting, "until they come to that place where the difference between the sacred and the secular cease to exist." "Our Fellow Christians" is the title of a message issued from the Fourth Assembly of the W.C.C. In it we are told that the purpose of the church is to "foreshadow a renewed human community." This renewed human community is seen producing 'a world tax system.'" This tax system "will demand the worship, discipline and mutual correction of the world-wide community." The W.C.C. is only "the beginning of this community."

When fully realized the one-church-for-one-world goal will mean the demise of the independence and autonomy of the local churches. Many of those presently affiliated with ecumenical organizations have already lost their autonomy. In time, however, the superchurch will completely order and regiment all of its constituents. The restructuring of the church, which ecumenists are now doing, is designed to abandon the traditional concepts of the church as a means of defending and proclaiming the gospel to one of dialogue with the world. In fact the world is to set the pace, write the agenda, for the church. Everything the

ecumenists do to advance the superchurch idea is in direct opposition to the Biblical concept of the universal Church and of
the local assemblies. Church unionism is hostile to local church
autonomy. The two cannot exist together. To achieve the one
is to surrender the other.

VI

EROSION FROM WITHIN

All is not well in the church-union drive. Without any attempt to present evidence for every form of erosion within the ecumenical empire, we will seek to expose some of the erosion as it exists in major denominations. Many who are in churches which are closely aligned and associated with either the N.C.C., W.C.C., or C.O.C.U., or even all three, are raising their voices in protest. What will result from these voices of protest, some of which are highly organized, only time will tell. Whether the erosion within the church-union efforts ever results in any major rift is open to serious question. One thing is sure though, church unionists are having trouble selling their bill of goods to many for whom they claim to speak. There is erosion within the empire. While the N.C.C., W.C.C. and C.O.C.U. leadership is calling for revolution of traditional and existing doctrine and structure in both church and state, sanctuary and society, there is a different kind of revolution going on against the church-union proposals on the lay level in many quarters of the home front.

News reporter, lecturer and author Will Oursler, viewing the liberal ecumenical movement as an ecumenical steam-roller, has this to say about the struggles going on within the movement: "A considerable degree of rebellion exists even among denominations active in the Council. There is opposition to what dissidents call 'this ecumenical steam-roller.' Strong dissident groups have sprung up in the Lutheran churches, in the United Presbyterian Church in the U.S.A. (Northern Wing) and the Presbyterian Church in the United States (Southern). There are dissident groups in the Northern Baptists and in the United Methodists."[39]

Presbyterian

One of the first serious forms of erosion within the liberal hierarchy determined to build a superchurch came from the National Lay Committee of the N.C.C. itself. The Committee was under the leadership of Mr. Jay Howard Pew. A 316-page document damaging to the N.C.C. for its political emphasis and neglect of spiritual ministries resulted. Because of its wide circulation, this document aroused concern and resistance on the part of many Christians in ecumenically affiliated denominations. Mr. Pew, who resigned from his post in the N.C.C. Lay Committee, wrote an article which was published in *Reader's Digest* exposing the misdirected efforts of the N.C.C. He took strong issue with the N.C.C. whose emphasis had shifted the responsibility of the church from one of the salvation of individuals to that of the reformation of society. In this provocative article, the question is asked "By what spiritual authority does this modern Christian church make this turn about from its ancient mission? Christ Himself made a clear distinction between the concerns of temporal and spiritual natures. He refused to immesh Himself or His followers in the economics, social and political problems of His day—problems certainly as serious as those we face today" (*Reader's Digest*, May, 1966). Ministers and laymen affiliated with churches in the N.C.C. and other ecumenical bodies have repeatedly reacted to pronouncements and resolutions of ecumenical enthusiasts. When church unionists have spoken out on

---

[39]Oursler, *op. cit.*, p. 9.

political issues and claimed to represent Protestantism, revolt has often resulted. Men have banded together to organize opposition to the liberal establishment, such things as the Free Church Association organized in California and the Committee of Christian Laymen of Savannah, Georgia. Numerous resolutions made against the National Council and the formation of many new denominations affixing the word "independent" before the old denominational label provide an array of evidence for erosion in the ecumenical empire.

In preparation of his most helpful book, *The Protestant Revolt,* James DeForest Murch made a survey of several hundred churches related to the N.C.C. but in the process of attempting to free themselves from it. This survey reveals something of the nature and extent of the unrest within the N.C.C. In response to ten basic questions regarding the responsibilities and actions of the church, it became evident how and why those who were affiliated with the N.C.C. sought to sever all relations with it.

An outstanding example of opposition from within the N.C.C. is in the "Prepared Statement" of Dr. Charles S. Poling delivered from the pulpit of the First Presbyterian Church of Phoenix, Arizona on February 12, 1961. This document received worldwide attention for its scathing accusations against the N.C.C. It was this paper which spearheaded the organization of the National Committee of Christian Laymen. Through an active campaign, Poling and others sought to alert other laymen of the involvement of their church in a massive "one-world Protestant church that theologically would be neither fish nor fowl, actually no church at all." The more this Presbyterian minister tried to reform from within, the more he came to realize the hopelessness of such a task. He found himself standing shoulder to shoulder with the avowed enemies of the Cross. Finally, he asked himself the question, "What can I do? As a Christian, I have no choice other than to separate myself from His foes and withdraw from a church that has been captured by liberal socialistic leaders, a church that has transferred her devotion and loyalty from Christ to the apostate anti-Christ, National Council of Churches."[40]

---

[40]Ingwalson, *op. cit.,* p. 243.

At the present time, there are two large reactions within Presbyterianism which speak out against the denominations' liberal tenets and their involvement with the N.C.C. Opposition to the new "Confession of 1967" gave rise to the first of these—*The Concerned Presbyterian Layman* published by the Presbyterian Lay Committee, Incorporated, and affiliated with the United Presbyterian Church, U.S.A. The Confession of 1967 really only made public what many Presbyterian clergymen believed and how they interpreted the old Westminster Confession all along. However, it did serve to arouse much concern on the part of hundreds of concerned Presbyterian laymen. A further reaction against the Presbyterian liberal establishment comes from the *Concerned Presbyterian* which is published by and gives voice to the conservative element in the Presbyterian Church, U.S. Related to the *Concerned Presbyterian* and supplementing it is an organization known as Concerned Presbyterians, Incorporated. Through this group's work, effort is being made to bring their church back to the primary mission of the church, the winning of the lost and the building up of the saints. While those responsible for these organizations and papers are still denominationally affiliated with the N.C.C., they do provide a sizeable erosion in the ecumenical empire.

Whether such opposition as outlined above does anything to stem the ecumenical tide remains to be seen. The issue is that there is opposition and erosion inside the ecumenical fold.

Lutheran

Lutherans associated with the ecumenical movement are also causing a ruffling of the ecumenical waters. Through its recent decision to declare pulpit and altar fellowship with the American Lutheran Church, the Lutheran Church—The Missouri Synod is indirectly associated with the ecumenical movement. This is true since the American Lutheran Church, third largest Lutheran body, is a member of the W.C.C. and will no doubt soon be also with the N.C.C. The Missouri Synod has refused to affiliate directly with the N.C.C. or the W.C.C. For many years, this church has stood for the orthdox Christian faith. In recent years, however, it has become obvious that an alarming number of the clergymen in the Synod no longer subscribe to belief in a totally inspired Bible. At least for the present, since it is now indirectly related to the church-union movement, the Lutheran Church—Missouri Synod does provide a genuine source of irritation. Irritation not only for more liberal-minded Lutherans, but also for the entire ecumenical movement. Like Presbyterians, Lutheran laymen are also organizing to oppose the political actions of their church according to the religious editor of the *Chicago Daily News*. Individual congregations, such as the Savior's Lutheran Church, Rich West, California are voting to sever relations with the Missouri Synod "because of the false doctrine being tolerated." This emphasis upon the existence of false doctrine in the Synod has been accelerated by the new relationship to the ecumenical movement via the American Lutheran Church.

United Methodist

The largest church merger in Protestant history involving some eleven million people took place with the formation of the United Methodist Church, April 21 — May 4, 1968. Both the Methodist Church and the Evangelical United Brethren Church were already members of the N.C.C., W.C.C. and the C.O.C.U. before their merger into the United Methodist Church. Before this merger took place, there was considerable opposition in both churches over theological liberalism and involvement in the ecumenical bodies. Again, laymen arose to protest. A classic example of such a revolt resulted in the production of a sixty-page brochure entitled "Things You Should Know About Subversive Influences in Methodism." Twenty Methodist laymen spelled out in unmistakable terms their strong opposition to the N.C.C. and their proposals for the recovery of their N.C.C.-affiliated church. Another Methodist laymen protest came with the Circuit Writers Incorporated. Here, too, in the purpose of this group, specific opposition was voiced against ecumenical and socialistic affiliation of the Methodist Church.

More recently, though, an unusual amount of erosion has been evident since the formation of the United Methodist Church.

Instead of producing harmony and unity, it produced friction and splits for many. In the states of Oregon and Washington alone, about half of the Evangelical United Brethren congregations planned to be absent for the final, really only formal, vote to unite the two churches. Fifty-one of the seventy-five churches of the Pacific Northwest Conference petitioned to withdraw because of the proposed merger; the churches withdrawing from the parent denomination expected to become a part of the new Evangelical Church of America. This group made it very clear that the reason for their action was because of their desire to retain their testimonial and Biblical position on the essentials of the faith. At considerable expense, such action was taken and is still being taken by brave and loyal Christians.

Baptist

Baptists have always held tenaciously to the right of soul liberty and the independent autonomous self-governing nature of the local church. When the Northern Baptist Convention, now the American Baptist Convention, became a member of the N.C.C. and the W.C.C., that Biblical principle of local church independence was flagrantly violated. Along with it, of course, the doctrine of soul liberty was virtually ignored. In fact, before the Convention became a part of the church-union drive, it had already usurped authority from the member churches, thus it was not difficult to take the next step and involve its churches in the liberal ecumenical machinery. That action caused much distress and strife. Numbers of churches from the beginning objected to such alignments. To this very day, many Baptist congregations which are officially a part of the ecumenical movement, by virtue of their being a part of the American Baptist Convention, are protesting vigorously. Undoubtedly, the most famous and most outstanding form of protest to date was the case of the First Baptist Church in Wichita, Kansas. After considerable dissatisfaction and subsequent investigation of the relationship between the N.C.C. and the American Baptist Convention, this church voted to withdraw from the Convention. A report of the findings of the lay committee was entitled "Why

One Church's Conscience Spoke Against the National Council of Churches." Convention officials forced the issue and made it necessary for the church to go to court to defend the action of the majority. The local court decided in favor of the majority. The Convention minority group appealed to the Kansas Supreme Court and won their case. Today, the new Metropolitan Baptist Church stands in Wichita, a two-million dollar plant which is experiencing phenomenal growth. The old Convention church is still there with only a small congregation and its old ties with the liberal American Baptist Convention and all the ecumenical trimmings besides. This Wichita story certainly reveals the fact of erosion within the superchurch goal.

Episcopalian

Controversy over involvements in ecumenical councils came to the fore in the Episcopalian Church recently because of the doctrinal beliefs and actions of the late Bishop James A. Pike. Since Pike was related to the Episcopal denomination and also with many of the left-wing theological and political pronouncements of the N.C.C., what he said caused many Episcopalians to rethink their view of the N.C.C. The confusion and controversy could not be kept quiet. Interest and contributions dropped off considerably in several areas. Various news media carried reports concerning revolt and erosion. The Rector of St. Thomas Church, Dr. T. Robert Ingram, voiced strong opposition to the N.C.C. In the *Houston Post*, he said the Council was "attempting to control American churches like a bee keeper uses the queen bee to control a swarming hive. The queen bee of the N.C.C. is one-worldism. They are all the time talking about world unity, one-world government, and a one-world church. Their line is indistinguishable from that of world communism in many respects. With the ruthlessness comparable to that of Russian communism, they are forcing American churches to go along on the party line. If you don't, you get stung."[41] An Episcopal Rector, Dr. Paul Kratzig, has also attempted to counteract the N.C.C. influence in his church. In addition to organizing a Foundation for Chris-

---

41 Murch, *op. cit.*, p. 125.

tian Theology, he has published a book entitled, *The National Council of Churches and the Social Revolution.*

The erosion evidenced by the revolt of the St. Marks Church in Shreveport, Louisiana was probably the most significant in the Episcopalian Church. Not only did the church take action to withdraw from the N.C.C., but it also called upon the diocese and the entire Protestant Episcopal Church to withdraw. This was not hasty action either. After a long study, an appointed committee recommended the action. The decision was based upon the finds of the committee concerning the liberal and subversive activists of the N.C.C. These instances of erosion in the Episcopalian Church are only examples of similar unrest in several other states. Such erosion within the ecumenical constituency must come as a hard blow to church-union enthusiasts.

Congregational

Even within the denomination which pioneered a plan for a united church, there has been and continues to be considerable erosion. The unrest and revolt was triggered by the formation of "The United Church of Christ" in 1957 through the merger of the General Council of the Congregational Christian Churches and the Evangelical and Reformed Church. At least two new fellowships have been formed in an attempt to gather together the scattered Congregational churches which opposed the merger for various reasons. These are The National Association of Congregational Christian Churches and the Conservative Congregational Conference. The latter of these two holds to a more rigid policy regarding the theological beliefs of its constituents than does the former. In addition to these, in attempting to minister to all concerned Congregationalists is the Committee for the Continuation of Congregational Christian Churches in the United States. Through the publication of many pamphlets and articles dealing with the dangers of the one-church-for-one-world idea, this dedicated group seeks to alert all Christians of the results of liberal ecumenism. The titles of the leaflets and fliers produced by this group are self-explanatory of their opposition to church unionism (i.e., *The Free Churches and the Ecumenical*

*Movement, The Ruthlessness of Church Union, The Mass Mind
and the Ecumenical Movement*). Through this media, many Congregationalists who are now a part of the United Church of Christ
and thereby very definitely related to the ecumenical movement
are being informed by their own brethren of the corruption in
the church-union drive. These informed people, in turn, often
leave the denomination and become a part of the new groups, or
they, at least, question the establishment regarding the one-
church program. Thus, there is erosion from this quarter also in
the ecumenical empire.

Orthodox Revolt

Newsweek, February 9, 1970, carried a lead article in the
religious section entitled "The Orthodox Revolt." The article
begins with these significant words: "Already under attack by
blacks, young activists and conservative Protestants, the National
Council of Churches last week was smarting from criticism from
yet another source: the nine Orthodox churches which are members of the ecumenical organization. Long out of sympathy with
the N.C.C.'s liberal stands on abortion, family planning and
black separatism, Orthodox bishops are privately re-evaluating
their relationship with the Council—including the possibility of
dropping out altogether."

The most recent criticism and evidences of revolt appear in
a critical memorandum prepared by theologians at St. Vladimir's
Orthodox Theological Seminary in Tuckahoe, New York. Their
charges center around the N.C.C.'s "hasty mergers and the dilu-
tion of Christianity in secularism." These Orthodox bishops ask
a very penetrating question and one which would not be expected
normally from an N.C.C. affiliate: "Is it Christian to unite with
those who are in fact the enemies of both Christianity and mankind?" The Dean of St. Vladimir's Seminary, Alexander Schmemann, was the first to present the memorandum at the biennial
meeting of the Standing Conference of Orthodox bishops in the
U.S. last October. Schmemann feels that regardless of the outcome of the memorandum, his own church, the Russian Metro-
polia in America, "is very close to leaving" the N.C.C. Even the

head of the Greek Orthodox Archdiocese of North and South America, Archbishop Iakovos, agrees with the memorandum "in its spirit." He feels though that withdrawal of the Greek Orthodox Church from the N.C.C. "is out of the question."

Whatever the final outcome, one thing is sure—there is plenty of uncomfortable revolt within the Orthodox Church over the N.C.C. and its ecumenical ties.

Summary

The purpose of this chapter has not been to make note of all the new denominations and organizations which have been formed in opposition to the ecumenical movement. These matters will be touched upon later. Rather, we have tried to illustrate here the widespread erosion which is taking place *within* those groups affiliated with the modern ecumenical movement. Several denominations have been cited as examples of groups which contain considerable amounts of this unrest. Other churches associated with ecumenical councils and endeavors have similar groups within their confines. Also, multitudes of individuals who are not as vocal and who are not a part of the organizations within denominations opposing church union must also be numbered among those erosive elements in ecumenism. Most often those lay people who favor the one-church-for-one-world idea are either unaware of what is happening and what its results will be and therefore are naive enough to believe the lie of the ecumenists, or they have not experienced personal salvation through faith in Christ as Sin-bearer and therefore are unable to understand the anti-biblical nature of such attempts and the will of God for them and for the church.

VII

OUTSIDE RESPONSE

It seems that laymen have a lack of knowledge of the large number of other Christians who are discontent with the church-union push. This is perhaps the greatest single factor contributing to the success of the ecumenical movement and the "What can we do?" attitude of evangelical Christians caught in the ecumenical web. This chapter concerns evangelical Christians outside the ecumenical empire. In the previous chapter we have tried to show something of the unrest on the part of many who, willingly or unwillingly, are a part of the drive for church union. Added to these there are millions of Bible-believers outside all the organizations striving for church union who are not in sympathy with the ecumenical program. A large number of denominations and churches not denominationally affiliated are at odds with the 'one-church-for-one-world' idea. What James DeForest Murch said about those outside the World Council of Churches also holds true for those outside the other liberal ecumenical organizations: "American Protestants numbering 30 million have refused to associate themselves with the World

Council. They contend that (1) it rejects an absolute minimum of Biblical doctrine as a basis for true Christian fellowship, (2) it is controlled by a liberal theological and sociological oligarchy, (3) it is beginning to function as a 'Super Church,' threatening the freedom of Protestant churches, (4) it is destroying distinctly evangelical Christian missions, (5) it is becoming more Catholic than Protestant, (6) it is encouraging leftist social revolution, meddling in national and international politics thus imperiling the status of the churches and the peace of the world, and (7) it is blurring the obligation of the Church Universal to maintain its apostolicity in doctrine, ordinances, and life by its emphasis on Christian unity for unity's sake and the building of One Church for One World."[42]

Though the Bible-believing Christians, whether denominationally aligned or not, do not agree on every point of doctrine they do hold much in common. They are in agreement on the essentials of the Christian faith. Some hold different views regarding the nature and extent of separation from the church-union movement and the enemies of historic orthodoxy than do others. They are agreed, however, on the inspiration and authority of the Bible and the full deity of the Lord Jesus Christ and the need for His salvation and lordship over a man's life. Belief in these things which matter most keep millions outside the ecumenical tent. Not only that, but among this number there are many who oppose the ecumenical attempts and are willing to "earnestly contend for the faith which was once delivered unto the saints."

In addition to religious responses there has always been response from those outside the ecumenical machinery and also outside the church itself. The strong civil reaction against the ecumenical movement cannot be ignored.

The response created by those outside then, the nonaligned, may be viewed from three major perspectives.

---

[42]Ingwalson, *op. cit.*, p. 210.

Religious Reactions

With the formation of the F.C.C. and the demise of the World Evangelical Alliance, fundamental Bible-believing Christians subsequently formed new organizations to promote Biblical Christianity. The motivations behind the formation of these new bodies was different; yet there was and remains general agreement on the unbiblical nature of the liberal ecumenical movement. One group attempted to take a purely positive approach, not seeking to organize evangelical Christians to be against anything, not even the existing liberal ecumenical church council. Others, however, felt it necessary to forthrightly oppose the liberal bodies. They thought a positive ministry of setting forth Biblical teaching was certainly necessary, but active opposition was also essential. The former of these two may be said to have reacted and the latter to have counteracted the prevailing church-union ambitions. It is with the former that we wish to deal here.

The desire for greater cooperation among evangelicals led to the formation of the National Association of Evangelicals.[43] "Cooperation without compromise" has been the theme of this association since it began in May, 1943 at Chicago. Those who led in its formation had specific complaints against the F.C.C. These they labeled a "bill of particulars." The "bill" accused the F.C.C. of refusing to adopt a basic minimal doctrinal statement. This allowed liberals to join who were definitely anti-Christian. Refusal of the Council to state clearly its belief in such important matters as the inspiration of the Bible and the deity of Christ made this possible. The F.C.C. was, even at that time, under the rule of an "oligarchy." Continuing their complaint, they said the F.C.C. was already acting as a "superchurch." Evangelicals also objected to the F.C.C.'s attacks against capitalism and its condoning of communism.

One of the past presidents of the N.A.E. set forth at one of the annual conventions the basic reason and purpose for its existence. Paul Petticord said that at its very inception the N.A.E. was: "(1) A spiritual movement born out of the desire and necessity for fellowship. (2) Formed as a result of the original Evan-

---

[43]Hereafter designated N.A.E. For list of constituency see Appendix D.

gelical Alliance from which liberals withdrew in 1894. (3) Not born to combat someone or some organizations, but to affirmatively make possible an organization for the declaration of the faith. (4) Not born to penetrate or infiltrate the National Council of Churches. (5) Not born to be an evangelistic agency but a fellowship that encourages and stimulates evangelism through or to the local church. (6) Not born to pre-empt the usage of the word 'evangelical' in place of 'fundamental.' (7) Not born to become one church in an organic sense nor to do the work of the church."44

This list reveals several important things about the N.A.E. It tells us primarily what the Association was *not* intended to be. These initial intentions of the early founders of the N.A.E. have been realized and perpetuated by the N.A.E. From the very start there was emphasis upon the fact that the N.A.E. was not intended to oppose the existing F.C.C. ecumenical council. Rather, the N.A.E. was designed to provide a means whereby evangelicals would join hands in Christian endeavor and a place where they could find a haven for Christian fellowship. The positive objectives of the N.A.E. have been set forth clearly by them: "1. To foster fellowship and good will among all Bible-believing Christians in line with the prayer of Christ, 'that they may be made perfect in one; and that the world may know that Thou hast sent Me.' 2. To provide a vehicle through which all believers in the Lord Jesus Christ may become united and articulate in matters of common interest and concern. 3. To establish a common front and a representation of evangelical interests, and the promotion of evangelical truth against the inroads of modernism in Christian institutions and in public life 4 To guard and promote religious freedom guaranteed us under our Constitution. 5. To provide our constituents with services which will enable them to accomplish more quickly and efficiently the speedy evangelization of the world."45

Emphasis is placed upon the strength of spiritual unity without organic union in the N.A.E. It seeks to provide such

---

44Paul P. Petticord, *True Ecumenicity* (Wheaton, Illinois: National Association of Evangelicals, n.d.) , pp. 9, 10.
45*The Strength of Spiritual Unity*, leaflet published by N.A.E.

4789 27

strength through a number of commissions and affiliated agencies. Exemplary of areas in which these operate would be Evangelism, Higher Education, Sunday School, Christian Day Schools, Publications, Foreign Missions, Women's Fellowship, Social Action, Radio and T.V. Broadcasting, Government Chaplaincy, World Relief, World Relations. The purpose and policy of the N.A.E. is reflected in these and other agencies. There is no attempt to expose or to oppose the ecumenical movement. The thrust of the N.A.E. and all its agencies is strictly an attempt to give a positive witness without a negative or strictly anti-ecumenical approach.

Perhaps the initial intention of insistence upon being purely positive and refusing to be *anti*-ecumenical, or *against* the F.C.C., explains several things which are true of the N.A.E. and its affiliates. Little wonder then that the decision regarding affiliation with liberal ecumenical organizations according to the N.A.E. remains with the individual. This means that in some cases a dual membership is possible. Affiliation with the N.A.E. and the N.C.C. is possible at the same time. This dual membership is true of some of the constituents of the N.A.E. A look at the roster of N.A.E. membership[46] reveals a rather wide divergence of doctrinal beliefs on some issues. The doctrinal statement of the N.A.E. which touches crucial areas of doctrine is certainly orthodox, though a bit incomplete in spots. Those affiliated with the N.A.E. must be in complete agreement with it. The statement is broad enough, however, to allow considerable difference of view in the areas of the doctrines of the Holy Spirit and last things. Another possible result of the "positive only" position of the N.A.E. is the fact that several of its constituent denominations are now on the "approved list" of the N.C.C. This means these denominations have applied for membership and are in line to become full-fledged members in the N.C.C. The N.A.E.'s original position may also account for the fact that its relief arm, the World Relief Commission, is presently cooperating with C.R.O.P., the relief arm of the W.C.C. One cannot help but wonder whether such a policy has not also led the N.A.E. to feature men

---

[46]See Appendix D.

like John Mackay, a member of the N.C.C. and a spokesman for church union, on its platform in 1968. The hesitatingly sympathetic attitude of the N.A.E. toward various ecumenical endeavors is disturbing to many, but it is not out of harmony with the original intention of the N.A.E. That original intention continues to be maintained. The Congress on Evangelism held in Berlin in 1966 was largely under the leadership and sponsorship of the N.A.E. The Ecumenical Press Service carried an interview between Evangelist Billy Graham and a W.C.C. official: "The World Congress on Evangelism does not want to be understood as being in opposition to the World Council of Churches, Dr. Graham said, but it is rather complimentary to it. It provides an opportunity for the more ecumenical evangelicals, many of those at the Congress belong to member churches of the World Council, some holding prominent positions in the World Council, to rub shoulders with other evangelicals, who wrongly think that being an evangelical means *ipso facto* to be in opposition to the World Council of Churches."

All of this leads one to agree with Harold Lindsell, editor of *Christianity Today,* in his words of warning to the 1969 N.A.E. convention when he said: "I would like to predict that within the next ten years there will be substantial changes that will take place among evangelicals. . . . And I'm speaking not about people outside the N.A.E., I'm speaking about evangelicals within the N.A.E." Lindsell went on to specify some of these changes: "For some years now, there has been going on among evangelicals an intra-party discussion about the most crucial issue of the Christian faith—the nature of inspiration and revelation. There has been some degree of attrition and deterioration in a theological sense in that direction. I forecast that within the next decade, there will be a further theological deterioration, particularly at the level of Biblical inerrancy. I think it's inevitable. What the outcome will be I do not know." Having said this, Dr. Lindsell predicted the very natural corollary between doctrinal deterioration and ecumenical involvement. He said, "I also foresee that many evangelicals will defect to the ecumenical movement and find a place for themselves within the structures of the World Council of Churches and the National Council of Churches. At the same time I believe that there will be a counter movement in the direction of the evangelicals outside the ecumenical movement from fellow evangelicals who are aligned with the ecumenical movement through their own ecclesiastical connections. All of this in turn suggests that within the next decade there will be some very substantial ecumenical realignment of various kinds."[47]

Possibility of closer relation between groups like the N.A.E. with the W.C.C. and other ecumenical endeavors in the future was anticipated and, it would seem, encouraged by Carl F. H. Henry, former editor of *Christianity Today,* in a dialogue with the W.C.C. leaders in the United States. He reviewed some reasons why evangelicals were not more involved with the W.C.C. and also spoke of ways whereby the W.C.C. could win more support from groups like the N.A.E.: "(1) Increase evangelical representation in World Council leadership. (2) Assign to the leadership of the W.C.C. committee on evangelism 'a majority' of Bible-oriented evangelical churchmen. (3) Restore the Bible 'to proper centrality in the churches' and as the norm for testing all pronouncements. (4) Encourage publishing houses to seek out Biblical material. (5) Represent articulate evangelicals on Protestant college campuses. (6) Renew 'moral conscience' among church-goers by emphasis on right conduct by men in public life" (*United Evangelical Action,* June, 1966, p. 19).

It seems apparent that there is a very close relationship between the original "positive only" rather than "anti-ecumenical" policy of the N.A.E. and the present desires and activities of the organization. The predictions for the future by some of the clientele of the N.A.E. also reveal the inevitable result of such an approach to the ecumenical movement.[48]

The reactionary policies of the N.A.E. in this country are represented by its sister organization operating on a world level—the World Evangelical Fellowship.[49] Bringing together seven national fellowships with twenty-one countries participating, the

---

[47]"The Future of Evangelicalism," a message delivered at the N.A.E. Convention, April 15, 1969.

[48]The neo-evangelical emphasis is discussed at length in the author's *Neo-Evangelicalism,* Fourth edition (Des Plaines, Illinois: Regular Baptist Press, 1971).

[49]Hereafter designated as W.E.F. For list of constituency see Appendix E.

W.E.F. was born in August, 1951. The doctrinal statements of the N.A.E. and the W.E.F. are almost identical. Purposes for existence are also the same for both groups, the major difference being that the W.E.F. seeks to represent evangelicals on a world level whereas the N.A.E. is a national organization. Policy regarding church-union movements is also the same with each group. While both organizations are not officially a part of the liberal ecumenical movement, both will permit their constituents to maintain membership in the N.C.C. or W.C.C. The W.E.F. also follows the N.A.E. policy of seeking to be positive without any intent or attempt to combat existing ecumenical councils, but rather to provide a place for evangelical fellowship and ministry. Because of the original purpose as well as the past and present practice of the N.A.E. and the W.E.F. they may legitimately be called reactionary movements. Without question, whether one agrees with these groups or not, they certainly represent a reactionary response to liberal church unionism.

Civil Reactions

Before looking at the counteractions against the one-church-for-one-world idea it will be profitable to note briefly something of the civil reactions to ecumenism. Increasing numbers of secular newspapers and magazines are carrying articles which reveal strong reaction to church unionism represented in the liberal ecumenical church councils. This has been true of a number of secular news media for some time, but there is an increasing emphasis upon it.

One of the outstanding civil reactions came when the W.C.C. invited communist clergy from behind the Iron Curtain to attend the Second Assembly of the W.C.C. meeting in Evanston, Illinois. The American Legion group from the Evanston area reacted strongly to the W.C.C. proposal. Without any denominational or theological ax to grind the American Legion voiced strong protest. The resolution which the Cook County Council of the American Legion passed was widely publicized and became general knowledge. The rather extensive resolution of the group emphasized that the bringing of communist clergy into this country was in violation of the spirit and even the letter of the McCarran-Walter Act. This act forbids the admission of such individuals into this country. Many others outside of the American Legion had raised serious questions regarding the admission of communist clergy into this country. In spite of much pressure to the contrary the State Department released the names of the communists who would be coming. Opposition to this decision was then voiced on the floor of the United States Congress. Alvin W. Bentley, Representative of Michigan, challenged the action of the Secretary in recommending that the eleven communist clergy be admitted. At the same time a large number of patriotic organizations in Chicago rented a hall and many people assembled to hear J. B. Matthews, a former chief investigator for the Committee on Un-American Activities, speak of the Reds in the W.C.C. Among other pointed and pertinent remarks he said, "If *ecumenism,* the watchword of Evanston, is broad enough to embrace agents of the Soviet conspiracy, then let *ecumenism* become a thing of 'hissing and a curse.' " Also, "If these clerics from Hungary and Czechoslovakia be emissaries of Jesus Christ, then let Christians restore Judas to his apostleship." This constitutes just a sample of the civil reaction to the world-church drive.

The same civil reaction continues today. Sadly enough, while most denominational papers are silent on the evils of ecumenism, and in fact seek to defend organizations like the N.C.C., the secular press reveals wariness with ecumenism. For example, the *Portland Oregonian* newspaper said recently in an editorial: "It is scarcely credible that the report of a study committee of the National Council of Churches whose 12 members are mostly ministers has endorsed the rise of violence to redress wrongs." The secular press is aware of the tremendous weakening in traditional religious beliefs which is so common in ecumenical circles. The *St. Louis Globe Democrat* for July 8 and 9, 1968 carried a story which revealed that some sociologists believe the current revolution in religion may spell the doom of the Christian church. Even a casual glance at almost any current newspaper or secular periodical designed to keep the public abreast of the current happenings will demonstrate the civil reaction to church unionism. Some of it is highly favorable to the ecumenical movement, but some of it is also very hesitant to fall for the ecumenical sales pitch.

Of course, the secular press on occasion also seeks to smear and belittle any who are not in sympathy with liberal ecumenism. *Look* magazine for April 24, 1962 illustrates this point. In an article entitled "The Rightist Crisis in Our Churches," Louis Cassels, United Press International religious writer, made strong attacks not only upon so-called religious rightists but also upon the chief of the F.B.I. itself as well as the President of the United States of America.

Such criticism is to be expected. What is so revealing though is not the fact that religious groups react to ecumenism or even that some outside the church criticize these religious groups. That which ought to cause deep concern for those involved in the one-church ambition is that even those outside the church, those who could hardly be called religious rightists, are seeing that beneath the superficial talk of being one in Christ there is a frightening and sickening ambition to build one church for one world.

Religious Countereactions

To react in relation to something is one thing. To counteract in relation to something is quite another. To react may simply evidence dissatisfaction, whereas to counteract reveals definite positive contradiction of and opposition to something. Two Councils of Churches, both in existence before the reactionary N.A.E. and the W.E.F., exist as definite counteractions against the liberal ecumenical movement. These two Councils—the American Council of Christian Churches,[50] organized on September 17, 1941 and the International Council of Christian Churches,[51] organized on August 11-19, 1948—both agree on a policy of opposition to the liberal ecumenical establishment as well as a positive proclamation of the faith once delivered unto the saints. Though under separate leadership, the I.C.C.C. purports to do internationally what the A.C.C.C. does nationally. Both Councils seek to counter

---

[50]Hereafter designated as A.C.C.C. For list of constituency see Appendix F.
[51]Hereafter designated as I.C.C.C. For list of constituency see Appendix G.

and oppose the work of the N.C.C. and the W.C.C. The doctrinal position of both groups is identical in all the essentials of the faith.

Liberal theology in general represented in the F.C.C. and especially in the Presbyterian Church U.S.A. gave rise to the A.C.C.C. Doctrinal impurities were evident for many years and in many areas. Famous orthodox men such as J. Gresham Machen, Robert Dick Wilson and Oswald T. Allis were forced to leave Princeton Seminary and founded Westminster Theological Seminary because of the liberal infiltration. The Reverend Carl McIntire, founder and first president of the A.C.C.C., was a student at the time of the conflict and left Princeton at the same time as the men mentioned above. The whole conflict came to a head over foreign missions. The presence of theological modernism was easy to demonstrate and to document on the mission field. After a series of conflicts with the denomination over its mission policies McIntire and others were defrocked because of their failure to obey the orders of their church. The Bible Presbyterian Church was formed as a result and McIntire became the pastor of one of its congregations in Collingswood, New Jersey.

Before organizing the A.C.C.C. those interested in its formation considered the possibility of reform within the F.C.C. After considerable thought and investigation they concluded that two basic facts made reform within the F.C.C. impossible. *First,* the fundamental structure upon which the F.C.C. rested was wrong. *Second,* the structure which had been erected on the platform was also in complete error. Since the A.C.C.C. is a council of churches, it began by getting individual churches to elect and send official delegates. The whole idea of a council to oppose the F.C.C. was discussed first by the Bible Protestant and Bible Presbyterian leaders. Committees were formed. They met and a proposed constitution was drafted and Carl McIntire was the first president. From the very beginning the line of separation between the F.C.C. and the A.C.C.C. was to be clearly drawn. Others soon joined the A.C.C.C. Immediately the A.C.C.C. began naming and opposing the F.C.C. It broke the monopoly of the F.C.C. in radio time, the military chaplaincy, Sunday School lessons and world day of prayer. Later on the I.C.C.C. was established to oppose the W.C.C. The A.C.C.C. was not intended to be a super-denomination. Nor has it ever attempted to be such. Democratic procedure has been the policy of the A.C.C.C. from its birth.

Before the organization of the N.A.E., discussed earlier, representatives from the A.C.C.C. attended the organizational meeting of the N.A.E. and they proposed that the N.A.E. unite with the already existing A.C.C.C. Some consideration was given to this proposal. But after due consideration it was deemed in-advisable. The major reason why these two groups of evangelicals did not join forces was because of the A.C.C.C.'s insistence upon complete separation from and active opposition to the F.C.C. As we noted earlier, the N.A.E. did not intend this as the purpose of its existence and does not consider it such today.

The unique and most basic purpose of the A.C.C.C. from its inception and as it exists today is to challenge the right of the F.C.C. (now N.C.C.) to speak for all Protestantism. The inclusion of the words *Christian* and *churches* into the name is very sig-nificant. Though the F.C.C. claimed to be Christian, it was so dominated by liberals that it was not representing historic Christianity. Too, even though it claimed to be a religious organ-ization, in reality it was only a social reform movement. The A.C.C.C. has not nor does it now hesitate to label the contempo-rary N.C.C. and W.C.C. as apostate. It refuses to permit any of its voting member churches to be related to these liberal church-union movements. In addition to the A.C.C.C.'s criticism of the theological liberalism in the ecumenical Councils it also accuses these organizations of being pacifistic and a threat to American freedom. Today the N.C.C. is viewed as soft and near commun ism as a result of its weak theological position. As far as the A.C.C.C. is concerned the N.C.C. is not even a truly Protestant council because of the inclusion of the Greek Orthodox Church in its membership and also because of its present flirtations and invitations to the Roman Catholic Church.

While it is true that the A.C.C.C. and the I.C.C.C. have con-centrated on opposing liberal ecumenical endeavors, it is also true that both Councils have always had a very positive ministry as well.[52] The stated position and purposes of each of these Councils is clearly set forth by their respective literature. The A.C.C.C.'s position and purpose presents both the positive and negative aspects of its work: "(1) To Provide a Pure Testimony for Fundamental Churches. (2) To Facilitate Cooperation among True Christian Churches. (3) To Project a United Stand against Religious Modernism. (4) To Expose Communist Infiltration into the Churches. (5) To Oppose Every System Alien to the Bible. (6) To Proclaim Unashamedly the Whole Counsel of God."

Unaffiliated either with those agencies viewed as reactionary or with those we have called counteractionary, many others nevertheless remain unaffiliated with the liberal ecumenical Councils. The Independent Fundamental Churches of America[53] is no doubt one of the outstanding examples of a fellowship of Bible-believing, anti-ecumenical individuals and churches not affiliated with any of the Councils mentioned above. This does not mean that the I.F.C.A. is not opposed to the ecumenical movement. Nor does it mean the I.F.C.A. is not in favor of what the evangelical church organizations are seeking to do. *The Voice* magazine, official organ of the I.F.C.A., regularly sets forth the position of the I.F.C.A. on these matters. At the present time at least the I.F.C.A., which now includes approximately 500 churches plus a large number of pastors, evangelists, missionaries, educators, and other full-time Christian workers, prefers to remain outside the N.A.E. and the A.C.C.C. Originally, the I.F.C.A. was a part of the A.C.C.C. In fact, it was one of the earliest groups affiliated with it. Without any change in its stand against the

---

[52]So have each of the groups associated with the A.C.C.C. had a very positive ministry. For example, the largest group and one of the earliest affiliates, the General Association of Regular Baptist Churches, has seen real growth since its initial withdrawal in 1932 from the old Northern Baptist Convention. At that time the Association started with twenty-two churches and at the last associational meeting in 1970 there were 1,400 churches affiliated with the Association. At the 1970 associational meeting the following report of giving was also presented: $8,044,806.32 for missions; $21,810,701.86 for current expenses; $5,508,083.90 for new buildings or additions to old ones. These facts demonstrate that proliferation can be and often has been healthy and that God honors and blesses those who obey Him.

[53]Hereafter designated as I.F.C.A. This organization is not made up of denominations or church bodies, but, as the name implies, independent, fundamental, Bible-believing churches in the United States.

ecumenical movement and for the fundamentals of the faith it withdrew from the A.C.C.C. The problem was related to personalities and not to doctrine. In reality, the doctrinal position and opposition to church unionism of the I.F.C.A. is identical to that of the A.C.C.C. In fact, the doctrinal statement goes further than the statement of either the N.A.E. or the A.C.C.C. by including belief in dispensationalism. This means that the I.F.C.A. requires its constituency to believe in a distinction between the nation Israel and the church. It holds that God has worked in different ways with His people through the unfolding of His program and that the present age is distinguishably different from the period of the law and from the future earthly kingdom to be established by our Lord. A distinction between the Church which is Christ's Body and the local church is also maintained. Other aspects of the I.F.C.A. doctrinal statement present a very definitive doctrinal position which clearly aligns the organization with the premillennial,[54] pretribulational[55] view.

The stated purpose, position, and policy of the I.F.C.A. places it in a position of counteraction against the ecumenical movement: "I. Our Purpose—the provision of a common ground of fellowship for churches and ministers that have separated from denominations which include unbelievers and liberal teachers; and, the encouragement of each other in the prosecution of God's program for world evangelization. We must never lose sight of the fact that men are lost and that our first business is soul-winning. II. Our Position—biblical separation: first, from apostate ecumenical movements of today, such as the National Council of Churches and secondly, from such carnality and worldliness as is condemned in the Word of God. III. Our Policy—the recognition of the sovereign, independent position of the local church in its own government. Our constitution does not permit any interference in the affairs of the local church by any officer of the national organization. However, the I.F.C.A. stands ready at

---

[54]Premillennial means Christ will return and establish His kingdom on earth.

[55]Pretribulational means Christ will return to this earth for His Church before the outpouring of God's wrath in the future seven-year Great Tribulation.

all times to give counsel or to lend assistance upon request of the local church."[56] There can be no mistake about it, the I.F.C.A.'s stated position is obviously not only a positive approach to the ecumenical problem. The organization takes a firm stand against ecumenism while at the same time it seeks to maintain a positive ministry. This relates the I.F.C.A. much more nearly to the work of the A.C.C.C. than it does to the N.A.E. Both the A.C.C.C. and the I.F.C.A. have very similar, if not identical, views regarding the essentials of the faith and the need for separation from apostasy. Counteraction against the church-union drive would be enhanced if the two groups would join forces.

A detailed study of the comparison between the number of Protestant churches not affiliated with the N.C.C. and the number of those affiliated with it yields some surprising results. Such a study, based on statistics in the *Yearbook of American Churches* was made recently by James DeForest Murch. His finds, considering a percentage of disaffected church members who oppose the N.C.C., indicated that presently there are more Protestants outside the N.C.C. than there are in the N.C.C. Added to this fact is the large number of varied agencies not officially aligned with the N.C.C. There are almost 300 mission agencies, dozens of institutions of higher education, hundreds of Protestant periodicals, and of course increasing numbers of religious radio broadcasts and radio stations without any relation whatsoever to the N.C.C. or its affiliates. Of course, not all of these agencies and their constituents share the same views regarding the ecumenical movement. However, they do represent a very significant number of Bible-believers whom the church unionists do not represent and for whom they cannot honestly speak. The outside response to the church-union movements is sizeable and causes great concern to the builders of one church for one world.

---

[56]Nye J. Langmade, *"P's" Do Tell the Story, Aims of the I.F.C.A.*, leaflet.

VIII

FACING FACTS

Certain things about the church-union movement are undeniable and indisputable. In the preceding chapters we have sought to deal with a number of crucial issues: the background of the ecumenical movement, outstanding landmarks along the way of its growth and development, confusion created by its propaganda, the goal of one church for one world, internal erosion, and response to the movement from outside. Now it is time to reflect on God's prediction of future judgment upon the world church and His message to His children for the present hour.

Ecumenism continues to be a subject of much debate in our day. Evangelical, fundamental Bible-believers are not all agreed on what the believer's attitude and approach to it should be. Doubtless there will continue to be much disagreement among Bible-believers. If those who profess to embrace the Bible as their only inerrant rule of faith and practice are consistent in that belief, however, certain things cannot be argued. It cannot be denied, whether one is obedient to the commands or not, that

Scripture does have much to say about false doctrine and the believer's responsibility to it. Nor can it be denied that the Bible predicts the existence and downfall of a world church and world government in the end times. These facts must be faced honestly by all who endorse and embrace the Bible as God's unerring Word.

Certain Collapse

Whether the contemporary church-union movement will succeed in building one church for one world remains to be seen. That there will be such a colossal church and empire in the future is very clear from the Bible. The certain collapse of that superstructure is also very clear. If the present-day ecumenical movement is not the organization which will eventually build the one church for one world, described in Holy Writ, then some other means will be used to accomplish it. All of the other signs of the time and of the end of the age seem to present evidence which would identify the church-union drive in our day as that vehicle by which the world church will be accomplished. The present-day ecumenical movement seems clearly to be preparing the way for the giant ecclesiastical structure supported by the civil government in existence during the future Great Tribulation. This will be a one-world church associated with a one-world government.

The declaration concerning the false religious system of the future is set forth by John, the Apostle, in these words: "And there came one of the seven angels which had the seven vials, and talked with me, saying unto me, Come hither; I will shew unto thee the judgment of the great whore that sitteth upon many waters: With whom the kings of the earth have committed fornication, and the inhabitants of the earth have been made drunk with the wine of her fornication" (Rev. 17:1, 2). In this inspired vision John receives information from one of the angels which had been used of God to pour out God's wrath upon men (Rev. 15, 16). This information concerns the divine description and destruction of the "great harlot."

Before attempting to identify the "great harlot" it would be well to present the order of events surrounding Revelation 17. Those who are truly God's children through faith in Jesus Christ as Savior are members of the universal Church called the Body of Christ (1 Cor. 12). All the members of this Church will be raptured from this earth to meet the Lord in the air and will forever be with Him (1 Thess. 4:13-18). Those who have truly been born-again and are a part of the ecumenical movement will be raptured along with those believers who are not a part of that movement. Yet, all those in all the churches, ecumenically or nonecumenically related, who were mere professors, without ever having been truly saved, along with all the other unsaved will experience a time of unprecedented trouble on the earth. The Bible speaks of this seven-year period as the time of Great Tribulation (Matt. 24:21 cf. Dan. 12:1). A detailed description of the kinds of judgments which God will pour out upon Christ-rejectors at that time is given in Revelation chapters 6-18. During this same period and immediately after the true Church is raptured, a false church becomes very prominent. It is so powerful that it controls the civil government for some time. Before Christ returns with His true Church to establish His kingdom on earth, the false superchurch will be destroyed.

A proper identification of the adulterous woman called the "great harlot" will show that this is a description of a future, false religious system. Elsewhere in the Book of Revelation religion is represented by the figure of a woman (2:20; 12:1; 19:7). Here, however, in 17:1 the reference is to false religion. The same false system is spoken of as a harlot three additional times in this same chapter (17:5, 15, 16). Such language is not uncommon in Scripture to describe departure from God's Word (Ezek. 16, 23; the Book of Hosea). This graphic description is used to emphasize the fact that the system referred to has been unfaithful to and has forsaken her original companion. That this "great harlot" is not the civil government is clear because it is with "the kings of the earth" that she commits fornication. The extent of the harlot's influence will be to "many waters" (17:2) or more literally, "peoples, and multitudes, and nations, and tongues" (17:15). Alliance of church with state will in that day enlarge and perpetuate the power of this false religious system.

Further description of the "great harlot" follows John's declaration of her influence: "So he carried me away in the spirit into the wilderness: and I saw a woman sit upon a scarlet coloured beast, full of names of blasphemy, having seven heads and ten horns. And the woman was arrayed in purple and scarlet colour, and decked with gold and precious stones and pearls, having a golden cup in her hand full of abominations and filthiness of her fornication: And upon her forehead was a name written, MYSTERY, BABYLON THE GREAT, THE MOTHER OF HARLOTS AND ABOMINATIONS OF THE EARTH. And I saw the woman drunken with the blood of the saints, and with the blood of the martyrs of Jesus: and when I saw her I wondered with great admiration. And the angel said unto me, Wherefore didst thou marvel? I will tell thee the mystery of the woman, and of the beast that carrieth her, which hath the seven heads and ten horns" (Rev. 17:3-7).

Here the harlot is seen sitting upon a beast. The color, names and description of this beast all serve to indicate its power and evil influence. By comparison of this beast with the one described in Revelation 13:1 there can be little doubt that they are the same. There (13:1) the beast receives his power from the dragon or Satan. Both the beast and Satan are worshiped. Through blasphemy and bloodshed this beast, who is usually seen to be a reference to a political ruler, also attempts to control religion as well. By contrasting the work of the first beast described in chapter 13 with that of the second one it seems clear that the first represents the political and the second the religious. The point John makes in his description of the "great harlot" in 17:3 is that she is riding upon this beast. In other words, the religious system is exercising power over political matters. The seven heads and ten horns of the beast speak of the confederated political kingdom which it represents. The Bible itself identifies the ten horns as ten kings (17:12) and the seven heads as the seven hills of the city of Rome which probably stand for seven Roman rulers (17:9).

Even the garments of the whore illustrate how the beautiful and symbolically pure and rich have been debased and prostituted by this false religious system (17:4). The depth and completeness of the whoredom of this system which makes an outward pretense of being godly is given clear presentation. She has in her hand a cup "full of abominations and filthiness of her fornication" (17:4).

The name on the forehead of the harlot provides further description of her identity and role. She, like the true Church (Eph. 5:32), is called a "MYSTERY" (17:5). Satan's work has always been to counterfeit the work of God, to mimic the genuine. "MYSTERY" also describes the concealed, the unknown, nature of the work of this religious system. This name also indicates that the reference to "Babylon" on her forehead does not mean the literal city but the religious system which that name represents. The political aspects of Babylon seem to be in view in chapter 18 of Revelation. Babylon had its beginning with the Tower of Babel in Genesis 10. The reference here by John is the climax of a long and error-filled system of religion called Babylon. "Babylon is actually a counterfeit or pseudoreligion which plagued Israel in the Old Testament as well as the church in the New Testament and which subsequently to apostolic days has had a tremendous influence in moving the church from Biblical simplicity to apostate confusion."[57]

Not only is this religious system spoken of as a "great harlot" but she is said to be the "MOTHER OF HARLOTS" (17:5). This means that she will include and involve in her sin all of apostate religion. "All apostate Catholicism, Protestantism, the cults, and pagan religions will be joined together in this amazing ecumenical organization of the end time. In order to accomplish unity it will be necessary to thrust aside all sound doctrine, and worse, this ecumenical organization will become the bitterest enemy of the saints, even to the point of becoming satiated with their blood (17:6)."[58] The relation between many of the practices of the Roman Catholic Church and the Biblical presentation of Babylon seems to point clearly to Roman Catholicism as the harlot. Yet while the Roman Church will undoubtedly be the center and major force in this future false religion, the picture

---

[57]John F. Walvoord, *The Revelation of Jesus Christ* (Chicago: Moody Press, 1966), p. 246.

[58]Herman A. Hoyt, *The End Times* (Chicago: Moody Press, 1969), p. 153.

presented here is broad enough to include all of apostate religion
in the end time. The language John uses here is all-inclusive.
Spiritual adultery is that which brings and binds the religions
of the world together.

After presenting detail concerning the beast (17:8-15) John
proceeds to outline the certain collapse or destruction of the
apostate religious system: "And the ten horns which thou sawest
upon the beast, these shall hate the whore, and shall make her
desolate and naked, and shall eat her flesh, and burn her with
fire. For God hath put in their hearts to fulfil his will, and to
agree, and give their kingdom unto the beast, until the words
of God shall be fulfilled. And the woman which thou sawest is
that great city, which reigneth over the kings of the earth" (Rev.
17:16-18).

Apparently God permits, for His own purpose, the world
church and the world government to use each other to accomplish their own ends. No doubt the beast and his confederacy,
represented in the heads and horns of the beast, find it necessary
to submit at least in part to the domination of the religious
system. Further study of the Book of Revelation makes it plain
that this will take place during the first half of the future Great
Tribulation. In an attempt to gain world power these govern-
mental rulers seek to utilize the power and prestige of the superchurch. When they have reached their goal they proceed to
destroy the religious system. Likewise, the superchurch had been
seeking to advance its cause by the use of civil and political
power. The withdrawal of all political and military support
from the superchurch takes place some time in the middle of the
Great Tribulation. The descriptive language used to speak of the
destruction of the religions by the political power emphasizes
how complete and final the collapse will be (17:16, 17).

Whether the current church-union move is the forerunner
of the future false church described in Scripture cannot be dog-
matically affirmed. Every indication points to the identity of the
two. Two things are certain and cannot be debated. First, leaders
of the current ecumenical movement have rejected the inerrant
authority of the Bible and are seeking to build a superchurch.
Second, the Bible predicts the existence of a flourishing false

superchurch before the second advent of Christ to establish His kingdom on earth.

Relating these certainties to contemporary church unionism reveals a striking similarity between the ecumenical movement of today and the superchurch of Revelation 17. Both are characterized by false doctrine and a rejection of the truth. Persecution and ridicule of those who maintain sound doctrine and are opposed to a superchurch is true of both. Involvement and inclusion of the Roman Catholic Church is obvious in both. Finally, alliance with and dependence upon the state characterizes both. If what we see today in the attempt for church union is the forerunner of what will become the superchurch, the false religious system of the future, then its collapse is certain. Lay involvement in the modern ecumenical movement will also take on a new perspective if this is true. The coming of the Lord must be very near.

Scripture, the Saint, and the Superchurch

Scripture speaks very plainly of a future false religious system. The destruction of that superchurch by the power of human government is equally as clear. Another fact, which cannot be avoided by the honest searcher of Scripture, concerns the Biblical commands upon the believer to separate from false doctrine. The evidence presented thus far may convince the reader that the church-union movement of our day is not Biblical. Perhaps it seems evident too that the contemporary church-union movement is preparing the way for the future false church which will be judged by God. Haunting the mind, the question may still linger, "But what should I do in relation to these things?" We have not attempted to deal with the believer's responsibility in light of the facts presented. Now that the church-union movement has been exposed for what it really is, what should the believer do? What should his attitude toward it be? God has not left His own without instruction concerning His desire for them in relation to their involvement in that which is not according to sound doctrine. Whether the false doctrine existed in ancient days or exists in our own day, whether it be embraced by an individual or an organization, the injunction of God's Word for the believer remains the same. The commands of God are not always easy to obey. Too often the Word of God is obeyed only if it is convenient. Many times clear and forthright Biblical instruction is subjected by us to our own prejudices and circumstances. If it suits us, we obey. If in the process of obeying we fear that we might lose friends or influence, the exhortations of Scripture are frequently disregarded.

The guidelines set forth here concern more than the matter of church unionism though that is our chief concern in this book. These Biblical principles relate to all and any form of false doctrine. Five great facts must be faced by all who subscribe and surrender to the inerrant authority of Holy Writ.

1. The Scriptural Prediction of False Doctrine

Our Lord often warned His own of many things. One of His greatest concerns for them was that they might be made aware of false teachers and false doctrine. Many of His comments regarding false teachers who would come in the future arose out of a context in which He was dealing with false doctrine and teachers of that day. Already in His day there were false prophets. Concerning these the disciples were warned because the false prophets were deceptive. They "come to you in sheep's clothing, but inwardly they are ravening wolves" (Matt. 7:15).

Paul, the Apostle, did not hesitate to warn the leaders of the church at Ephesus concerning the coming of "grievous wolves." He had the "flock" or congregations over which the elders had oversight in mind. He feared for them. There was no question in his mind that after his departure these false teachers would "enter in among you, not sparing the flock." For this reason he warned the pastors and commended them to the sovereign care of God (Acts 20:28-32). The Holy Spirit gave the same great Apostle a similar concern for the believers at Corinth. He feared that just as the serpent beguiled Eve, so the minds of the Corinthians would be "corrupted from the simplicity that is in Christ" (2 Cor. 11:3, 4). There was no doubt in his mind that there were those who were preaching "another Jesus." This was his same concern for the saints in the church at Galatia. Some of the believers there were following after "another gospel" (Gal. 1:6). Some false teachers even in Paul's own day had already succeeded in "bewitching" the Galatians so that they would not obey "the truth" (Gal. 3:1). The "gospel" these false teachers were preaching was another gospel of a different kind. It was a false gospel and not the gospel of Christ. Under the inspiration of God Paul could therefore pronounce an anathema, "let him be accursed," upon such.

With dogmatic certainty the young preacher Timothy was told that "in the latter times some shall depart from the faith" (1 Tim. 4:1). Instead of declaring the doctrines of God they give heed to the "doctrines of devils." Timothy was told also that in the last days many would have only "a form of godliness" (2 Tim. 3:1-4). Hymenaeus and Alexander had already "made shipwreck" of the faith in Paul's day (1 Tim. 1:19, 20). Lest Timothy fall into similar error he was warned to take heed.

The saints addressed in the Book of Hebrews were also alerted to the presence of false doctrine in their day. In the midst of general instruction concerning holy living the writer said, "Be not carried about with divers and strange doctrines" (Heb. 13:9). Truth was constantly under attack because of the presence of error. The Apostle Peter reminded the scattered and persecuted saints to whom he wrote that their day was not much different from Old Testament days at least in one particular. There were "false prophets" among their forefathers and there would be "false teachers" among them (2 Pet. 2:1). John, the beloved disciple, firmly but graciously told the saints, "Beloved, believe not every spirit, but try the spirits whether they are of God: because many false prophets are gone out into the world" (1 John 4:1).

Even a surface reading of Scripture brings one face to face with the issue of false doctrine. It was already present when the New Testament was being written and it was predicted as a certainty for the future. Close examination of these and many other texts reveals that the kind of false doctrine spoken of revolves around a false view of the living Word—Jesus Christ—and the written Word—the Bible. These have always been centers of controversy, and they remain the most crucial doctrines of the Christian faith.

2. *The Scriptural Principle of Separation*

Truth and error are always separated in Scripture. They are opposites which will not admit of synthesis with God. Scripture speaks of them as mutually exclusive. God is the epitome of truth as Satan is of error. From the very beginning God separated light from darkness. Throughout Scripture darkness speaks of error and light speaks of truth, and the two are diametrically opposed to each other. "God is light, and in him is no darkness at all" (1 John 1:5). The children of God are to bear family resemblance. They are constantly to avoid error by walking in the light. It goes without saying that the children of God are to refrain from sin. Scripture makes that abundantly clear. Since departure from and denial of the faith are certainly sin it follows that believers are to refrain from aligning themselves with that departure. Severe judgment of God is pronounced upon those who profane the name of God or the cause of God. Rejection of the inerrant authority of Scripture and the deity of Christ certainly profanes the name and cause of God. That the liberal ecumenical establishment has repudiated these and many other basic Christian doctrines has already been established. It remains for the believer to understand that alignment with the ecumenical movement or even inclusion in the numbers which church unionists use to accomplish their ends makes him party in one way or another to that which he rejects and which God will one day judge.

God's people have throughout Scripture been marked as a distinct, peculiar and separated people. Jehoshaphat, king of Judah, was rebuked by God for lending assistance to the wicked despisers of God and His people (2 Chron. 19:2). The law of God to His own made it explicit that they should "not plow with an ox and ass together" (Deut. 22:10). Surely this was designed to teach them the law of separation. That which was to characterize their physical lives was also to be true of the spiritual life. This principle was stated by God to His own in the form of a question, "Can two walk together, except they be agreed?" (Amos 3:3). It is simply impossible to have true Biblical fellowship with those who deny the very essentials upon which that fellowship is made possible. This does not mean believers are to hate and avoid all who are not born-again. Such an attitude would militate against the very reason for the believer's existence—to propagate the gospel and glorify God. Personal friendship is one thing. Fellowship involving union and the joining of hands for a so-called Christian effort with those who reject the orthodox Christian faith is another.

3. The Scriptural Command to Separate

Not only does the Bible predict that false teachers and doctrine would come but it gives guiding principles regarding the believer's relation to these things. Scripture also contains clear, specific and forthright proclamation instructing the child of God not to fellowship with the "unfruitful works of darkness" (Eph. 5:11). The word *fellowship* carries the idea of being "a joint partner with." The command of God is clear then. The believer is not to get himself mixed up with false doctrine. Instead he is to "reprove" such (Eph. 5:11). This exhortation can only be completely obeyed by separation from false teachers and doctrine, God has pronounced a curse upon those who proclaim a false gospel (Gal. 1:8, 9). How then can a child of God find fellowship and cooperation with that which stands under the judgment of God. To join hands in a Christian endeavor with those who repudiate and scoff at the living and written Word of God is to form an unequal yoke or bond. Scripture warns against such an association. It gives the reasons too, " . . . For what fellowship hath righteousness with unrighteousness? and what communion hath light with darkness? And what concord hath Christ with Belial? or what part hath he that believeth with an infidel?" (2 Cor. 6:14, 15). In the context of this forceful passage the issue centered in heathen idols and the Corinthians' responsibility to be apart from them. The principle of separation from error cannot be removed from the passage though. Here are broad and all-inclusive statements which apply to any culture and circumstance where truth and error are involved. The command cannot be argued: "Wherefore, come out from among them, and be ye separate, saith the Lord . . . " (2 Cor. 6:17).

Paul's exhortation to Timothy, his young son in the faith, was very similar to that which he gave the Corinthian believers. "From such withdraw thyself," he told Timothy (1 Tim. 6:5). Again the reason for separation centered in a false doctrine concerning Jesus Christ. His command to "turn away" from those which have only a form of godliness but deny its power cannot mean anything else (2 Tim. 3:5). Furthermore, the phrase "turn away" is in the present tense and imperative mood. That means it is a command for a continuous turning away from false doctrine. There is no option provided here. Timothy's friends, family, or circumstances have nothing to do with the divine imperative regarding separation from error. Earlier in the same letter a similar exhortation appears. Those who name the name of Christ are to "depart from iniquity" (2 Tim. 2:19). Those who promote false doctrine are likened to vessels of dishonor. When the believer purges himself from such, he is then a "vessel unto honour, sanctified, and meet for the master's use . . . " (2 Tim. 2:21). The word "purge" used in the passage means to "clean thoroughly." This demands separation. Titus was given the same command. A "heretic" or factious person he was to "reject" (Titus 3:10).

John, the Apostle of love, had some strong words regarding the believer and false doctrine. His chief concern was in the Person and work of Christ. Said he, "Whosoever transgresseth, and abideth not in the doctrine of Christ, hath not God. He that abideth in the doctrine of Christ, he hath both the Father and the Son" (2 John 9). Such words are most applicable to the church-union movement. As we pointed out earlier, many ecumenists no longer even try to hide their rejection of the historic, orthodox and Biblical doctrine of Christ. John's command follows his description of the false doctrine: "If there come any unto you, and bring not this doctrine, receive him not into your house, neither bid him God speed" (2 John 10). Perhaps John was referring to one of the house churches which were prevalent in his day. Or he could have meant a family abode. Either inter-

pretation fits the context. At any rate, the command is clear:
Do not receive a false teacher into your house and do not bid
him God's blessing. The reason for the command follows: "For
he that biddeth him God speed is partaker of his evil deeds" (2
John 11). After the destruction of the future superchurch spoken
of as Babylon, the Spirit of God extended an invitation to the
true people of God. It is an invitation to separate from that
which God has condemned: "Come out of her, my people, that
ye be not partakers of her sins, and that ye receive not her
plagues" (Rev. 18:4).

The issue of separation from apostasy is settled for the
Bible-believer. He really has no choice in the matter if he would
obey God's Word. God has spoken on the subject. The believer
is now responsible to obey.

Many evangelicals who are still in some way a part of the
church-union effort would agree with the foregoing. They believe the Bible teaches separation from apostasy even though
they, for varied reasons, have not yet completely severed ties with
it. An even more difficult truth for many to accept and obey is
that Holy Scripture commands separation from Christian brethren who persist in walking in disobedience. As in the case of
separation from apostasy and false teachers this does not mean
each believer is to set up his own beliefs as equivalent to God's
truth. God's Word and the essentials of the faith constitute that
from which there can be no deviation, and these must be the
norm by which our views are to be judged.

Though difficult to understand and sometimes even more
difficult to obey, God's Word addresses itself to the question of
a believer's fellowship with another believer who persists in disobedience and specific sins. The Corinthian Christians were told
bluntly to "put away from among yourselves that wicked person"
in their assembly who was guilty of gross sin and who refused to
confess it (1 Cor. 5:13). The "wicked person" is described as one
who is called a brother and is guilty of fornication, coveteousness
and drunkenness, among other things (1 Cor. 5:9-11). Again to
the saints at Thessalonica the Apostle wrote definitely: "Withdraw yourselves from every brother that walketh disorderly, and
not after the tradition which he received of us" (2 Thess. 3:6).

Here the issue was doctrinal. Professed believers seem to be in view in Paul's words to the Christians at Rome: "Mark them who cause divisions and offences contrary to the doctrine which ye have learned; and avoid them" (Rom. 16:17). The Apostle insisted that his inspired messages concerning the Lord Jesus Christ allowed for no deviation. Christ is crucial to Christianity; in fact, without the Christ of Scripture Christianity does not exist.

All that the Scripture has to say regarding a given subject must be taken into account in arriving at its exact teaching on that particular matter. This is just as true in the doctrine of separation from false teaching as it is in any other area. It is altogether too easy and common to attempt to "prove" something from the Bible by simply marshaling "proof texts," often taken out of context, and failing to consider all that Scripture has to say on the subject.

It cannot be denied that each time Scripture speaks about false doctrine it does not always include a command to separate from it. On different occasions false doctrine is exposed by the writer and demonstrated to be false, but all such exposures of error are not accompained with a command for the believer to separate from it. Some in the assembly at Corinth said there was no resurrection from the dead (1 Cor. 15:12). The church at Thessalonica was plagued by word and letter to believe that they were already in the Day of the Lord and thus had missed the Rapture (2 Thess. 2:2). Paul sought to correct both of these errors, but in neither case did he encourage the believer to immediately withdraw from the assemblies because of the errors. As has been demonstrated, there are a significant number of passages which clearly do command the believer not to be party to false doctrine. Too, it has been seen that this is the general principle in God's Word even when not specifically stated. How often does God have to say something before it becomes a command? Do we have a right to expect God to repeat such commands each time error is exposed? Other doctrines are not treated that way in Scripture. For example, we do not deny the deity of Christ just because that truth is not clearly stated and stressed each time truth about the Person of Christ is given. The truth of His deity is often clearly given and therefore must be believed even though that truth is not repeated each time reference is made to Him. It is the same way with the doctrine of separation.

Another word of caution is in order lest we become unbiblical in our desire to be Biblical. Too often we become careless, unbalanced, self-centered, and thus unscriptural in our attempt to obey the Word of God. Especially is this true when trying to reach decisions and provide answers for some very real questions: How extensive must the apostasy be before separation is necessary? What doctrines are crucial to the faith and thus the ones which will not allow for compromise and differences? Who determines when men or movements have embraced false doctrine? When does a church or other organization become apostate? Such questions are not always easy to answer. Certain general principles do provide guidelines for answering them under all circumstances. During the closing years of the nineteenth century and the early years of the twentieth when the battle was beginning to rage between fundamentalism and modernism, five great fundamentals were set forth as the measuring rod to determine whether one was fundamental in the faith or whether he embraced theological modernism. These five fundamentals of the faith were forged out of concentrated Bible study and Bible conferences. They were: (1) the virgin birth of Christ, (2) the substitutionary atonement of Christ, (3) the deity of Christ, (4) the bodily resurrection of Christ from the dead and His Second Coming, and (5) the inspiration of Scripture (the term *inspiration* was then used as a synonym for inerrancy—that the Bible was without error in all its pronouncements).

These are still the criteria by which to establish whether an individual or an organization is orthodox or heterodox. Other doctrines might be listed as equally essential to the faith. What is believed about these, however, will reveal what is believed about other Biblical truths. They are determinative! A glance at these five historic fundamentals of the faith reveals that they all center around two crucial doctrines, the very two which liberal church unionists of our day deny in any orthodox sense—the doctrines of Christ, the living Word and the Bible, the written Word. Of course, contemporary Bible-rejectors often disguise their rejection with orthodox-sounding words. Therefore, it is often necessary to understand what is meant by the use of these terms. Deviation from the Biblical teaching on any one of these means a movement away from truth to error. Separation of the believer is thus imperative! A good rule by which to determine when a church, denomination, or other organization becomes apostate or embraces false doctrine and thereby making it necessary for believers to separate from it is to consider the officials or policy makers. If the official leadership does not in truth subscribe to the fundamentals of the faith, the believer has no choice but to sever connections and break off fellowship with such because he really has nothing in common that is essential to the faith. The official creeds or doctrinal statements of the group may, and in most cases do, sound quite orthodox. Yet the very ones who profess to believe them and the ones who determine the group's affairs often repudiate all the essentials of the faith. Ordination vows and assent to traditional statements of faith are meaningless to such individuals.

Leaving one's church or refusing to be a part of some church effort because of the presence of false doctrine is not always an easy decision to make. Family, friends, and long-time associations often make the decision to obey God's Word even harder. There are always bound to be those who do not understand and who are quick to accuse the separatist of having a holier-than-thou attitude and of being too concerned about so-called minor things. Those who attempt to obey the Biblical doctrine are even often accused of not believing in evangelism and fellowship with other Christians. Francis Schaeffer stated the issue bluntly when he said: "Thus it must be said that in spite of (and even because of) one's commitment to evangelism and co-operation among Christians, I can visualise times when the only way to make plain the seriousness of what is involved in regard to a service or an activity where the Gospel is going to be preached is *not* to accept an official part, if men whose *doctrine* is known to be an enemy are going to be invited to officially participate. In an age of relativity the *practice* of truth when it is costly is the only way to cause the world to take seriously our protestations concerning truth. Co-operation and unity that do not lead to purity of life and purity of doctrine are just as faulty and incomplete as an orthodoxy which does not lead to a concern for, and a reaching out towards, those who are lost."59

4. The Scriptural Attitude in Separation

Too often separatists forget that the Biblical doctrine of separation is both positive and negative. The time sequence of these opposites is imperative. Unless there is first of all separation *unto God,* all separation *from apostasy* will be meaningless. The scriptural commands to "contend for the faith" (Jude 3), to "hold fast the form of sound doctrine" (2 Tim. 1:13) refer to the body of truth committed to us and not to our own personal views. This requires complete dedication to the Lord and His Word. Determination to defend an organization or one's own views often replaces the command to contend and "continue in the faith" (Col. 1:23) and to abound in the "work of the Lord" (1 Cor. 15:58).

Opposition to and separation from something is often accomplished by a lack of love, humility, and prayer toward those ensnarled in false doctrine. Human nature is such that it is easier to lash out at someone than it is to love, easier to be harsh and to hate the erring one than it is to be humble in spirit, easier to pronounce judgment than it is to pray for those in error. Yet Scripture clearly reveals that we are to exercise love for those from whom we separate, love for God and His truth, and not for our own selves (1 Tim. 1:5). Prayers are to be made for "all men," even those who hold false doctrine and oppose God's Word (1 Tim. 2:1). Humility is to characterize those who seek to restore one "overtaken in a fault" whatever that fault may be (Gal 6:1)

Because some fail to manifest love, prayer, and humility as they preach and practice separation from false doctrine, an erroneous connotation has been created in the minds of many. Unfortunately, separation from false doctrine is not seen as a Biblical doctrine because surely a loveless, prayerless, and proud attitude is not. True, a bitter and harsh attitude, a failure to pray

---

59Francis Schaeffer, *The God Who Is There* (Chicago: Inter-Varsity Press, 1968), p. 169.

for enemies of Christ, and pride are wrong. But because these attitudes are sometimes associated with some who separate from apostasy does not make the doctrine of separation unbiblical. What is needed in these days of church-union attempts and widespread adherence to false doctrine is simple obedience to the commands of God—obedience not only to separate from these but also to be completely separated unto God. This in turn will create within the separatist the Biblical attitudes of love, prayer, and humility. The fact is, the commands of Scripture to separate are not completely obeyed until these qualities characterize the believer. Paul put it bluntly when immediately after his exhortation against false doctrine he said, "Now the end of the commandment is charity [love] out of a pure heart, and of a good conscience, and of faith unfeigned" (1 Tim. 1:5).

5. *The Scriptural Purpose of Separation*

Granted, if the Bible teaches separation from false doctrine, the believer who claims the Bible as his rule of faith and practice has no choice but to obey. If God commands it, we must comply or we are disobedient. But are there any other answers to the question, Why separate?

There are a number of Biblical purposes. Beyond the necessity of simple obedience there is the blessed privilege of honoring God and His Word by obedience. Compliance with the exhortation of Scripture to separate also provides a means of defending the doctrinal purity of the church and its testimony. This is not to say that it is possible to have a perfect church. It is not. Maintenance of sound doctrine in the assembly is certainly a Biblically warranted endeavor. In fact, the bonafide existence and ministry of the church demands that it remain true to the Word of God. When it departs from the Word, it has no genuine and unique reason to exist. Other organizations can, and do, serve for the good of mankind in various social activities and probably do it better than the church. Christians are to be like salt in the earth. Among other things this implies that believers are to exert a preservative and preventative influence in the world. The Holy Spirit desires to work through God's children to restrain sin—

to hold it in check. Such a ministry cannot be fully effective when compromise and alliance is made with those opposed to the Bible and other essentials of the faith. Too, some erring brethren can be restored and helped when the command to separate is obeyed. Many new and immature Christians look to older more mature ones for guidance. As long as those who know the Biblical injunctions do not share them with others and do not obey them themselves, many "babes in Christ" are led astray. We all have a testimony to bear before God and others. No amount of rationalization and excuses will clear us before the Lord when we have failed to obey what He clearly revealed and is known by us. To summarize, separation from false doctrine makes it possible for the believer and his church to do and to be precisely what God intends for them to do and to be—shining lights for Jesus Christ in a sin-darkened world. Assisting the enemy of the Cross in no way honors Jesus Christ, the Commander-in-Chief.

IX

SUMMARY

What can be done about the modern church-union movement? Since conditions and trends such as we see now are predicted for the last days of the church, surely the ecumenical movement cannot be stopped. Why get concerned about it then? Why fight it? Is not fighting against it a losing battle? If it is a part of God's sovereign will, are we not opposing Him when we oppose the ecumenical attempts to build a world church? There are some evangelicals who attempt to hide under God's sovereignty and say since the Bible predicts departure from the faith and a colossal religious system in the end time, therefore believers should not busy themselves opposing such things. The fallacy of such thinking is that it ignores the clear command of Scripture to "Fight the good fight of faith . . . " (1 Tim. 6:12), and to "earnestly contend for the faith . . . " (Jude 3). Then, too, what would become of the Christian life in general if such an approach were taken toward it? The Bible is clear in its pronouncements of the certainty of satanic opposition against the believer and of the persistent harassment of satanic forces seeking to overthrow the child of God. Does this mean the Christian is simply to give up and succumb to the Devil because evil opposition is promised? Not at all! Scripture is equally clear in its command to "put on the whole armour of God" and wage active combat against Satan and all his forces even though God allows them to come to the believer. Likewise, even though God in His sovereignty is permitting the church-union movement and all the apostasy associated with it to prevail, yet the child of God is commanded to oppose it and separate from it.

Our study has brought several crucial issues to our attention: (1) The modern church-union movement is dominated by those who deny the cardinal doctrines of the historic Christian faith. The most crucial doctrines which are denied are the doctrines of the inspiration of the Bible and the absolute deity of Christ. Rejection of these leads very naturally to the rejection of other essentials of the faith. (2) Today the ecumenical movement is being advocated and advanced by the N.C.C., the W.C.C. and the C.O.C.U. (3) Total confusion characterizes the church-union efforts. Words are invested with new meanings. Church union is said to be the greatest good and denominational division the greatest evil. Strangely enough, Scripture which is divested of divine authority is used to support ecumenical efforts. Christianity and communism are confused. The central role of the church has shifted from the proclamation of God's truth to correction of social ills and the creation of a world government by which the future world church can function. (4) The goal of church unionists is to build a monolithic superchurch. (5) Unrest and unhappiness exists on the lay level inside the ecumenical empire. (6) Evangelicals have responded in opposition to the liberal ecumenical efforts by forming councils of churches and associations of evangelicals to break the liberal monopoly. (7) Scripture predicts the creation and downfall of a superchurch. It also gives clear instruction regarding the believer's responsibility toward false doctrine.

That which concerns Bible-believers most about the modern church-union movement is its total disregard for God's truth. Truth matters to people of the Book. It cannot be treated lightly. Those who love God's written Word take their stand with God's living Word when He said, "thy word is truth" (John 17:17). Evangelical Christians are not opposed to efforts to understand each other more or to joining hands with those of like precious faith to present a common front for the Savior and against sin and unbelief. Neither are they disturbed at the thought of those who reject the Christ of Scripture and the Scripture of Christ all joining in one great religious organization. What they are rightly concerned about though is for that union of unbelievers to purport to speak for Christians and to include those who love Christ in their confines.

One of the major purposes of this book has been to awaken the Christian public to what is happening to the churches. It is hoped that this purpose has been realized and that acquaintance with the facts has raised in the reader's mind the legitimate question, What can I as an individual do about the liberal ecumenical church-union movement? Based upon what has been presented in this volume, especially in chapter 8, here are some practical suggestions of what you can do:

1. Pray that God will give you wisdom, courage, and grace to obey His Word concerning your affiliation with the liberal ecumenical movement and your rejection of it.

2. Pray for those who are involved in the church-union movement, especially those who know and love the Lord and His Word that they might see the need to stand on God's side.

3. Promote Bible study and prayer groups in your home and community.

4. Acquaint yourself with the facts related to the drive for church union. Be open to these even if it involves you and/or your church.

5. Know what the Bible teaches concerning the denial of the faith in the last days and the believer's responsibility in light of it.

6. Ask your pastor or denominational leaders what your church's official position is regarding crucial doctrines of the faith such as Christ and the Bible. Ask them also

what your church's position is relative to the ecumenical movement.

7. Withdraw your support and membership from all organizations which are related to and a part of the liberal church-union movement.

8. Become a part of and an active member of a Bible-believing, Bible-preaching local church.

9. If there is not a thoroughly evangelical, fundamental church in your community, enlist the help of a nearby evangelical pastor or evangelical school to start one.

10. Seek to inform your Bible-believing friends about what is happening to the churches.

11. Combat ecumenism by word of mouth and by distributing factual literature which exposes it.

12. Support with your prayers and finances those organizations such as churches and schools which are in opposition to the ecumenical movement and are seeking to present a positive testimony for Biblical truth.

13. Keep abreast of current happenings in the modern church-union movement by reading literature which favors it and literature which exposes and opposes it.

14. Show genuine love and concern to and for those ensnarled in ecumenism. Be a consistent witness for Christ by allowing the fruit of the Spirit to be manifest in your life.

The contemporary church-union movement is not a layman's effort. This volume is intended, though, to inform concerned laymen of what church unionism is all about and what they can do about it. What the layman does will not stop the reckless drive for one church for one world, but it will result in the blessing of God because of obedience to the Word of God. Now it is time for the man in the pew to stand up and be counted for the cause of Christ.

APPENDICES

APPENDIX A

World Council of Churches Constituency[*]

Sinodo Evangelico Aleman del Rio de la Plata (Evangelical German Synod of Rio de la Plata) — Argentina
Methodist Church of Australasia
Church of England in Australia
Congregational Union of Australia
Federal Conference of Churches of Christ in Australia
Presbyterian Church of Australia
Evangelical Kirche A.U.H.B. in Oesterreich (Evangelical Church of the Augsburg and Helvetic Confession) — Austria
Old Catholic Church in Austria
Lesotho Evangelical Church — Basutoland
Eglise Chretienne Missionnaire Belge (Belgian Christian Missionary Church)
Eglise Evangelique Protestante de Belgique (Evangelical Protestant Church of Belgium)
Episcopal Church in Brazil
Igreja Metodista do Brasil (Methodist Church of Brazil)
Federacao Sinodal, Igreja Evangelica de Confissao Lutherana no Brazil (Synodal Federation, Evangelical Church of Lutheran Confession in Brazil)
Bulgarian Orthodox Church (Eglise orthodoxe de Bulgarie)
Burma Baptist Convention
Eglise Evangelique du Cameroun (Evangelical Church of Cameroon)
Eglise Presbyterienne Camerounaise (Presbyterian Church of Cameroon)
Presbyterian Church in West Cameroon

---

[*]As of March 1968.

Union des Eglises Baptistes du Cameroun (Union of Baptist Churches of Cameroon)
The Anglican Church of Canada
Churches of Christ (Disciples) — Canada
The Evangelical Lutheran Church of Canada
Presbyterian Church in Canada
United Church of Canada
Yearly Meeting of the Society of Friends — Canada
The Church of the Province of Central Africa
The United Church of Central Africa in Rhodesia
United Church of Zambia
The Methodist Church in Ceylon
Iglesia Evangelica Luterana en Chile (Evangelical - Lutheran Church in Chile)
Iglesia Pentecostal de Chile (Pentecostal Church of Chile)
Mision Iglesia Pentecostal (Chile) (Pentecostal Mission Church)
China Baptist Council
Chung-Hua Chi-Tu Chiao-Hui (Church of Christ China)
Chung Hua Sheng Kung Hui (Church in China)
Hong Kong Council of the Church of Christ in China
Hua Pei Kung Li Hui (North China Congregational Church)
Disciples du Christ au Congo (Disciples of Christ in Congo)
Eglise Evangelique du Congo (Evangelical Church of the Congo)
Eglise Evangelique Manianga Matadi (Manianga Matadi Evangelical Church)
Church of Cyprus
Ceskobratska Cirkev Evangelicka (Evangelical Church of Czech Brethren)
Ceskoslovenska Cirkev (Czechoslovak Church)
Evangelicka Cirkev A.V. Na Slovensku (Evangelical Church in Slovakia, Augsburg Confession)
Orthodox Church of Czechoslovakia
Ref. Cirkev Na Slovensku (Reformed Christian Church in Slovakia)
Slezska Cirkev Evangelicka A.V. (Evangelical Church of the Augsburg Confession in Silesia)
Baptist Union of Denmark

Den Evangelisklutherske Folkekirke I Danmark (Church of Denmark)

Church of the Province of East Africa

Presbyterian Church of East Africa

Coptic Evangelical Church — The Synod of the Nile

Coptic Orthodox Church — Egypt

Greek Orthodox Patriarchate of Alexandria — Egypt

Ethiopian Orthodox Church

Suomen Evankelis-Luterilainen Kirkko (Evangelical Lutheran Church of Finland)

Eglise de la Confession d'Augsbourg d'Alsace et de Lorraine (Evangelical Church of the Augsburg Confession in Alsace and Lorraine) — France

Eglise Evangelique Lutherienne de France (Evangelical Lutheran Church of France)

Eglise Reformee d'Alsace et de Lorraine (Reformed Church of Alsace and Lorraine) — France

Eglise Reformee de France (Reformed Church of France)

Eglise Evangelique du Gabon (Evangelical Church of Gabon)

Altkatholische Kirche in Deutschland (Old Catholic Church in Germany)

Evangelische Brueder Unitaet (Moravian Church) — Germany

Evangelische Kirche in Deutschland (Evangelical Church in Germany)

> Evangelische Kirche in Berlin-Brandenburg
> Pommersche Evangelische Kirche
> Evangelische Kirche von Schlesien
> Evangelische Kirche der Kirchenprovinz Sachsen
> Evangelische Kirche von Westfalen
> Evangelische Kirche im Rheinland
> Evangelisch-Lutherische Landeskirche Sachsens
> Evangelisch-Lutherische Landeskirche Hannovers
> Evangelisch-Lutherische Kirche in Bayern
> Evangelisch-Lutherische Kirche in Thueringen
> Evangelisch-Lutherische Landeskirche im Hamburgischen Staate
> Evangelisch-Lutherische Landeskirche Schleswig-Holsteins
> Evangelisch-Lutherische Landeskirche Mecklenburgs

Braunschweigische Evangelisch-Lutherische Landeskirche
Evangelisch-Lutherische Kirche in Luebeck
Evangelisch-Lutherische Landeskirche von Schaumburg-
  Lippe
Evangelische Landeskirche in Wuerttemberg
Evangelisch-Lutherische Kirche in Oldenburg
Evangelisch-Lutherische Landskirche Eutin
Evangelische Kirche in Hessen und Nassau
Evangelische Landeskirche von Kurhessen-Waldeck
Evangelische Landeskirche in Baden
Vereinigte Protestantische Kirche der Pfalz
Evangelische Landeskirche Anhalts
Bremische Evangelische Kirche
Evangelisch-Reformierte Kirche in Nordwestdeutschland
Lippische Landeskirche
Vereinigung der Deutschen Mennonitengemeinden (Mennonite
  Church) — Germany
Evangelical Presbyterian Church — Ghana
The Methodist Church — Ghana
Presbyterian Church of Ghana
Ekklesia Tes Ellados (Church of Greece)
Greek Evangelical Church
A Magyarorszagi Evangelikus Egyhaz (Lutheran Church of Hun-
  gary)
A Magyarorszagi Reformatus Egyhaz (Reformed Church of Hun-
  gary)
Baptist Church of Hungary
Evangelical Lutheran Church of Iceland
Church of India, Pakistan, Burma and Ceylon
Church of South India
Federation of Evangelical Lutheran Churches in India
Mar Thoma Syrian Church of Malabar — India
Orthodox Syrian Church of the East — India
The Samavesam of Telugu Baptist Churches — India
United Church of Northern India
Geredja Geredja Kristen di Djawa Tengah (Christian Churches
  in Mid-Java) — Indonesia

Geredja Gereformeerd di Indonesia (Reformed Church in Indonesia)

Geredja Kalimantan Evangelis (Evangelical Church in Kalimantan) — Indonesia

Geredja Kristen Djawa Wetan (Christian Church in East Java) — Indonesia

Geredja Kristen Indonesia (Indonesian Christian Church)

Geredja Kristen Pasundan (Sundanese Christian Church of West Java) — Indonesia

Geredja Kristen Sulawesi Tengah (Christian Church in Mid-Sulawesi) — Indonesia

Geredja Masehi Indjili di Minahasa (Christian Evangelical Church) — Indonesia

Geredja Masehi Indjili Timor (Christian Evangelical Church in Timor) — Indonesia

Geredja Protestan di Indonesia (Protestant Church in Indonesia)

Geredja Protestan Maluku (Protestant Church in the Moluccas) — Indonesia

Geredja Roradja, Toradja Church, Indonesia (Reformed)

Huria Kristen Batak Protestant (Protestant Christian Batak Church) — Indonesia

Synod of the Evangelical Church of Iran

Chiesa Evangelica Metodista d'Italia (Evangelical Methodist Church of Italy)

Chiesa Evangelica Valdese (Waldensian Church)

The Presbyterian Church of Jamaica

The United Church of Jamaica and Grand Cayman

Nippon Kirisuto Kyodan (United Church of Christ in Japan)

Nippon Sei Ko Kai (Anglican Episcopal Church in Japan)

Greek Orthodox Patriarchate of Jerusalem

Korean Methodist Church

Presbyterian Church in the Republic of Korea

Presbyterian Church in Korea

Armenian Apostolic Church

Evangelical Synod of Syria and Lebanon

Union of the Armenian Evangelical Churches in the Near East

Church of Christ in Madagascar

Eglise des Amis a Madagascar (Malagasy Friends Church)

Eglise Evangelique de Madagascar (Evangelical Church of Madagascar)

Malagasy Lutheran Church

Iglesia Metodista de Mejico (Methodist Church of Mexico)

Algemene Doopsgezinde Societeit (General Mennonite Society) —
Netherlands

Bond van Vrije Evangelische Gemeenten in Nederland (Union of
Free Evangelical Congregations) — Netherlands

Evangelisch Lutherse Kerk (Evangelical Lutheran Church) —
Netherlands

Nedersland Hervormde Kerk (Netherlands Reformed Church)

Oud-Katholieke Kerk (Old Catholic Church) — Netherlands

Remonstrantse Broederschap (Remonstrant Brotherhood) —
Netherlands

Eglise Evangelique en Nouvelle-Caledonie et aux Iles Loyaute
(Evangelical Church in New Caledonia and the Loyalty Isles)
— New Caledonia

Presbyterian Church of the New Hebrides

Geredja Kristen Indjili di Irian Barat (Evangelical Christian
Church in West Irian — Reformed)

Associated Churches of Christ in New Zealand

Baptist Union of New Zealand

Church of the Province of New Zealand (Church of England)

Congregational Union of New Zealand

Methodist Church of New Zealand

Presbyterian Church of New Zealand

The Methodist Church — Nigeria

Presbyterian Church of Nigeria

Norske Kirke (Church of Norway)

United Presbyterian Church of Pakistan

Iglesia Catolica Filipina Independiente (Philippine Independent
Church)

United Church of Christ in the Philippines

Eglise Autoceph. Orthodoxe en Pologne (Orthodoxe Church of
Poland)

Kosciol Ewangelicko-Augsburski w Polsce (Evangelical Church of
the Augsburg Confession)

Kosciol Polskokatolicki w.P.R.L. (Polish-Catholic Church in Poland)

Evangelical Synodal Presbyterial Church of the Augsburg Confession in the People's Republic of Rumania

Biserica Evangelica Dupa Confesiunea Dela Augsburg (Evangelical Church Augsburg Confession) — Rumania

Biserica Ortodoxa Romane (Rumanican Orthodox Church)

Biserica Reformata din Romania (Transylvanian Reformed Church) — Rumania

Congregational Christian Church in Samoa

Bantu Congregational Church in South Africa

Bantu Presbyterian Church of South Africa

Church of the Province of South Africa

Congregational Union of South Africa

Evangelical Lutheran Church in Southern Africa — South East Region

Methodist Church of South Africa

Moravian Church in the Western Cape Province — South Africa

Presbyterian Church of Southern Africa

Iglesia Evangelica Espanola (Spanish Evangelical Church)

Svenska Kyrkan (Church of Sweden)

Svenska Missionsfoerbundet (Mission Covenant Church of Sweden)

Christkatholische Kirche der Schweiz (Old Catholic Church) — Switzerland

Schweizerischer Evangelischer Kirchenbund — Federation des Eglises Protestantes de la Suisse (Swiss Protestant Church Federation)

Greek Orthodox Patriarchate of Antioch — Syria

Syrian Orthodox Patriarchate of Antioch and all the East — Syria

Eglise Evangelique de Polynesie Francaise (Evangelical Church of French Polynesia)

Tai-Oan Ki-Tok Tiu-Lo Kau-Hoe (Presbyterian Church in Formosa)

Evangelical Church of North Western Tanganyika — Tanzania

Evangelical Lutheran Church in Tanzania (Kanisa la Kiinjili la Kilutheri Tanzania)

Usambara-Digo Lutheran Church — Tanzania

Church of Christ in Thailand

Eglise Evangelique du Togo (Evangelical Church of Togo)
Presbyterian Church in Trinidad
Ecumenical Patriarchate of Constantinople — Turkey
The Church of the Province of Uganda and Rwanda Burundi
Baptist Union of Great Britain and Ireland
Churches of Christ in Great Britain and Ireland
Church of England
Church of Ireland
Church of Scotland
Church in Wales
Congregational Union of England and Wales
Congregational Union of Scotland
Episcopal Church in Scotland
Methodist Church — U.K. and Eire
Methodist Church in Ireland
Moravian Church in Great Britain and Ireland
Presbyterian Church of England
Presbyterian Church in Ireland
Presbyterian Church of Wales
The Salvation Army — U.K. and Eire
Union Welsh Independents (Congregational)
United Free Church of Scotland
African Methodist Episcopal Church — United States of America
African Methodist Episcopal Zion Church — United States of America
American Baptist Convention
The American Lutheran Church
Christian Methodist Episcopal Church—United States of America
Church of the Brethren — United States of America
The Church of the East (Assyrian) — United States of America
Evangelical United Brethren Church — United States of America
Hungarian Reformed Church in America
International Convention of Christian Churches (Disciples of Christ) — United States
Lutheran Church in America
The Methodist Church — United States of America
Moravian Church in America (Northern Province)
Moravian Church in America (Southern Province)

National Baptist Convention of America

National Baptist Convention, U.S.A., Inc.

Polish National Catholic Church of America

Presbyterian Church in the U.S.

Protestant Episcopal Church — United States of America

Reformed Church in America

The Religious Society of Friends — United States of America
  Friends United Meeting
  Friends General Conference

Romanian Orthodox Episcopate of America

Russian Orthodox Greek Catholic Church of America

Seventh Day Baptist General Conference — United States of America

Syrian Antiochian Orthodox Church (Archdiocese of New York and all North America)

United Church of Christ — United States of America

United Presbyterian Church in the United States of America

Armenian Apostolic Church — U.S.S.R.

Estonian Evangelical Lutheran Church — U.S.S.R.

Evangelical Lutheran Church of Latvia — U.S.S.R.

Georgian Orthodox Church — U.S.S.R.

Orthodox Church of Russia, Patriarchate of Moscow

Union of Evangelical Christian Baptists of U.S.S.R.

The Church of the Province of West Africa

Methodist Church in Sierra Leone

Anglican Church of the West Indies

Reformed Christian Church of Yugoslavia

Serbian Orthodox Church — Yugoslavia

Slovak Evangelical Church of the Augsburg Confession in Yugoslavia

Eesti Ev. Lut. Usu Kiriku (Estonian Evangelical Lutheran Church in Exile)

Lietuvos Ev. Reformatu Baznycia (Lithuanian Reformed Church)

The Conference of the Methodist Church in the Caribbean and the Americas

APPENDIX B

*National Council of Churches Constituency**

A. *Member Churches*

African Methodist Episcopal Church
African Methodist Episcopal Zion Church
The American Baptist Convention
Antiochian Orthodox Catholic Archdiocese of Toledo, Ohio
    and Dependencies
Armenian Church of North America: Eastern Diocese, West-
    ern Diocese
Christian Church (Disciples of Christ)
Christian Methodist Episcopal Church
Church of the Brethren
Church of the New Jerusalem
The Episcopal Church
Exarchate of the Russian Orthodox Church of North and
    South America
Friends United Meeting
Greek Orthodox Archdiocese of North and South America
Hungarian Reformed Church in America
Lutheran Church in America
Moravian Church in America
National Baptist Convention, U.S.A., Inc.
National Baptist Convention of America
Philadelphia Yearly Meeting of the Religious Society of
    Friends
Polish National Catholic Church of America
Presbyterian Church in the U.S.
Progressive National Baptist Convention, U.S.A., Inc.
Reformed Church in America
Romanian Orthodox Episcopate of America
Russian Orthodox Greek Catholic Church of America
Serbian Eastern Orthodox Church
Seventh Day Baptist General Conference
Syrian Antiochian Orthodox Church

---

*As of this publication.

Syrian Orthodox Church of Antioch
Ukrainian Orthodox Church of America
United Church of Christ
The United Methodist Church
United Presbyterian Church in the U.S.A.

NOTE: In addition to the above there are twenty-seven denominations which are "eligible for membership." This means they are eligible to have persons serving on some of the committees within the Council. The names of these denominations are not released.

B. *U.S.A. member churches which are also members of the W.C.C.*

African Methodist Episcopal Church
African Methodist Episcopal Zion Church
American Baptist Convention
The American Lutheran Church
Christian Church (Disciples of Christ)
Christian Methodist Episcopal Church
Church of the Brethren
The Church of the East (Assyrian)
The Episcopal Church
Hungarian Reformed Church in America
Lutheran Church in America
Moravian Church in America (Northern Province)
Moravian Church in America (Southern Province)
National Baptist Convention of America
National Baptist Convention, U.S.A., Inc.
Polish National Catholic Church of America
Presbyterian Church in the U.S.
Reformed Church in America
The Religious Society of Friends
Friends United Meeting
Friends General Conference
Romanian Orthodox Episcopate in America
Russian Orthodox Greek Catholic Church of America
Seventh Day Baptist General Conference
Syrian Antiochian Orthodox Church

United Church of Christ
The United Methodist Church
United Presbyterian Church in the U.S.A.

C. *Organizations in Fraternal Relationship*
National Council of the Young Men's Christian Associations of the U.S.A.
National Board of the Young Women's Christian Associations of the U.S.A.
General Commission on Chaplains and Armed Forces Personnel
U.S. Conference for the World Council of Churches
American Bible Society
Council of Community Churches

NOTE: The above six organizations were previously recognized by the Council as organizations in fraternal relationship and invited to name fraternal delegates to both the General Assembly and General Board.

D. *Organizations in Fraternal Relationship to Divisions*
Agricultural Missions, Inc.
American Associate Board of St. Christopher's Training College, Vepery, Madras, Inc.
American Association of Theological Schools
American Friends Service Committee
American Leprosy Missions, Inc.
American McAll Association
American Youth Foundation
Armenian Missionary Association of America, Inc.
Associate Board of Women's Christian College, Madras, Inc.
Association of Council Secretaries
Canadian Council of Churches
Christian Children's Fund, Inc.
Committee on Christian Literature for Women and Children in Mission Fields, Inc.
Congo Inland Mission, Inc.
Cooperative Publication Association
Council of Hispanic-American Ministries
Heifer Project, Inc.

International Christian Youth Exchange
International Society of Christian Endeavor
International Student Service (formerly Committee on Friendly Relations Among Foreign Students)
Japan International Christian University Foundation, Inc.
John Milton Society
Koinonia Foundation
Laymen's Overseas Service, Inc.
Lott Carey Baptist Foreign Mission Convention
Ludhiana Christian Medical College Board, U.S.A.
Lutheran Orient Mission Society of America
Mennonite Central Committee
National Conference on Christian Work Among Chinese in America
National Women's Christian Temperance Union
New York City Mission Society
Santal Mission
Society for Propagating the Gospel Among the Indians and Others in North America
United Board for Christian Higher Education in Asia
Vellore Christian Medical College Board, Inc. (North American Section)
Volunteers of America
World Council of Christian Education and Sunday School Association
Yale-in-China Association, Inc.

APPENDIX C

Consultation on Church Union Affiliates*

African Methodist Episcopal
African Methodist Episcopal Zion
Christian Methodist Episcopal
Disciples of Christ
Episcopal

---

*As of this publication.

Presbyterian
United Methodist
United Church of Christ

APPENDIX D

*National Association of Evangelicals Membership**

A. *Denominations*
   Assemblies of God
   Baptist General Conference
   Brethren in Christ
   Christian Church of North America
   Christian and Missionary Alliance
   Christian Union
   Church of God (Cleveland, Tenn.)
   Church of the United Brethren in Christ
   Churches of Christ in Christian Union
   Conservative Congregational Christian Conference
   Elim Missionary Assemblies
   Evangelical Church of North America
   Evangelical Congregational Church
   Evangelical Free Church of America
   Evangelical Mennonite Brethren Church
   Evangelical Mennonite Church
   Evangelical Methodist Church
   Free Methodist Church
   General Conference of the Brethren Church
   Holiness Methodist Church
   International Church of the Foursquare Gospel
   International Pentecostal Assemblies
   Mennonite Brethren Church
   Midwest Congregational Christian Fellowship
   Missionary Church Association
   National Association of Free Will Baptists
   Ohio Yearly Meeting of Friends

------

*As of this publication.

Open Bible Standard Churches
Oregon Yearly Meeting of Friends
Pentecostal Church of Christ
Pentecostal Church of God
Pentecostal Evangelical Church
Pentecostal Holiness Church
Primitive Methodist Church
Reformed Presbyterian Church of North America
Rocky Mountain Yearly Meeting of Friends
United Fundamentalist Church
United Missionary Church
Wesleyan Church

B. *Individual Churches From*

American Baptist Convention
Berean Fundamental Churches
Bible Churches
Bible Baptist Churches
Christian Reformed Church
Church of the Brethren
Church of the Nazarene
Community Churches
Conservative Baptist Association
Disciples of Christ
English Lutheran Church
Evangelical Covenant Church
Free Baptist Churches
General Association of General Baptists
General Conference Mennonite
Grace Brethren Churches
Independent Churches
Independent Baptist Churches
Independent Presbyterian Churches
Kansas Yearly Meeting of Friends
Methodist Church
North American Baptist Churches
Presbyterian Church in the U.S.
Reformed Church in America

Southern Baptist Convention
United Baptist Churches
United Presbyterian Church in the U.S.A.

C. *Associations and Organizations*

Anchor Bay Evangelistic Association
Association of Fundamental Ministers and Churches
Full Gospel Church Association
Grace Gospel Evangelistic Association
National Holiness Association
New England Evangelical Baptist Fellowship
New England Fellowship of Evangelicals
Advent Christian Church, N. Calif. Conf.
Advent Christian Church, Massachusetts Conf.
Advent Christian Church, New Hampshire Conf.
American Association of Evangelical Students, Inc.
Bethany Fellowship, Inc.
Bible Literature International
Gospel Association for the Blind
National Negro Evangelical Association
Overseas Christian Servicemen's Centers, Inc.
Protestant Religious Education Services, Inc.
The Railroad Evangelistic Association
The World Home Bible League

APPENDIX E

*World Evangelical Fellowship Membership**

The Evangelical Alliance — Britain
The Evangelical Fellowship of Canada
Evangelical Alliance Ceylon
China Evangelical Fellowship — Taiwan
Evangelisk Alliance i Danmark — Denmark
Alliance Evangelique Francaise — France
Deutsche Evangelische Allianz — Germany
The Evangelical Fellowship of India

---

*As of this publication.

Evangelical Alliance (Canterbury) — New Zealand
Okinawa Evangelical Fellowship
Fraternite Evangelique du Senegal — Senegal
Sierra Leone Evangelical Fellowship
The Evangelical Fellowship of the South Pacific Islands
Hoi Tin Lanh Tong Cong Viet Nam — South Vietnam
Alianza Evangelica Espanola — Spain
Schweizerische Evangelische Allianz — Switzerland
National Association of Evangelicals — U.S.A.
Evangelical Fellowship of West Pakistan

APPENDIX F

*American Council of Christian Churches Membership**

Bible Presbyterian Church
Bible Protestant Church
Congregational Methodist Church
Evangelical Methodist Church
Fundamental Methodist Church
General Association of Regular Baptist Churches
Independent Bible Baptist Missions
Independent Fundamental Bible Churches
Methodist Protestant Churches
Southern Methodist Church
South Carolina Baptist Fellowship
Tioga River Christian Conference
Ukrainian Evangelical Baptist Convention
World Baptist Fellowship
United Christian Church

NOTE: Not every church in these denominations is a member
of the A.C.C.C. An individual church vote is usually
required. However, most of the churches affiliated with
these independent denominations are also members of
the A.C.C.C. by separate vote.

---

*As of this publication.

APPENDIX G

*International Council of Christian Churches Constituency**

Bolivian Evangelical Church
Brazilian Evangelical Christian Church
Churches of World Missions, Inc. — Brazil
Conservative Presbyterian Church of Brazil
Federation of Regular Baptist Churches, N. E. Brazil
British Guiana Congregational Union
Conservative Regular Baptist Association of Canada
Free Christian Reformed Church — Canada
Convencion de Iglesias Bautistas de la Mision Chilena — Chile
Evangelical Presbyterian National Corporation — Chile
Alliance Church of Christ in China
China Church of Christ
Free Methodist Church — China
Gospel Church of Christ in China
Ling Liang Churches — China
Northwestern Federated Church of Christ — China
Presbyterian Church of Christ in China
Evangelical Methodist Church in Guiana — Surinam
Bible-believing Church of Formosa
China Presbyterian Church of Christ in Taiwan
Union des Associations Cultuelles Evangeliques des Eglises Methodistes de France
Polish Reformed Church in Exile — England
Bible Presbyterian Church of India
The Christian Evangelical Mission — Indonesia
Irish Evangelical Church, Ireland
The Presbytery of Western Africa in Liberia
Christian Reformed Churches — Netherlands
Evangelical Church of the Moluccas — Netherlands
Reformed Churches of New Zealand
Zion Methodist Church — Nigeria
Association de Iglesias Bautistas de la Selva — Peru
Presbyterian Church of Ayacucho and Huancavelica — Peru

---

*As of this publication.

Association of Baptist Churches on Luzon — Philippines
Bukidnon Association of Baptist Churches — Philippines
Palawan Association of Baptist Churches — Philippines
Visayan Fellowship of Fundamental Baptist Churches—Philippines
The Defender of the Faith Churches — Puerto Rico
Swedish Alliance Mission — Sweden
The United Church — Thailand
Associated Gospel Churches — U.S.A.
Bible Presbyterian Church — U.S.A.
Conference of Fundamental Churches — U.S.A.
Eastern Conference of the Bible Protestant Church — U.S.A.
Evangelical Methodist Church — U.S.A.
Free Magyar Reformed Church in America
Fundamental Conference of America, Inc.
General Conference of the Methodist Protestant Church—U.S.A.
Independent Bible Baptist Missions — U.S.A.
Independent Churches Affiliated with the I.C.C.C. — U.S.A.
Independent Fundamental Methodist Church, Inc. (Mo.)
International Conference of Calvary Tabernacles — U.S.A.
Militant Fundamental Bible Churches — U.S.A.
Southern Methodist Church — U.S.A.
Tioga River Christian Conference — U.S.A.
United Christian Church — U.S.A.
World Baptist Fellowship — U.S.A.

APPENDIX H

Selected Bibliography

The following books all expose the church-union movement. Each one is written from a different perspective, and the authors do not all agree on what should be done about the drive for church union. All do not agree either on what the individual believer should do who is affiliated with a church which is involved in the ecumenical movement. However, all do agree that the intended purpose of the ecumenical enthusiasts is to build a superchurch. They also agree that the drive for one church for one world is being pushed by ecumenists who do not accept the

Bible as the unerring Word of God or Jesus Christ as the very Son of God — God manifest in the flesh.

Brown, Harold O. J. *The Protest of a Troubled Protestant.* Grand Rapids: Zondervan Publishing House, 1970. 282 pp. Paper.

Hedegard, David. *Ecumenism and the Bible.* London: The Banner of Truth Trust, 1964. 236 pp. Paper.

Ingwalson, Kenneth W. (compiler). *Your Church—Their Target.* Arlington, Virginia: Better Books Publisher, 1966. 275 pp. Paper.

Kik, J. Marcellus. *Ecumenism and the Evangelical.* Philadelphia: Presbyterian and Reformed Publishing Company, 1958. 152 pp. Hard cover.

Lowell, C. Stanley. *The Ecumenical Mirage.* Grand Rapids: Baker Book House, 1967. 205 pp. Hard cover.

Montgomery, John Warwick. *Ecumenicity, Evangelicals, and Rome.* Grand Rapids: Zondervan Publishing House, 1969. 107 pp. Hard cover.

Murch, James DeForest. *The Protestant Revolt.* Arlington, Virginia: Crestwood Books, 1967. 328 pp. Paper.

Oursler, Will. *Protestant Power and the Coming Revolution.* Garden City, New York: Doubleday and Company, Incorporated, 1971. 203 pp. Hard cover.

INDICES

SUBJECT INDEX

SCRIPTURE INDEX